MW00939697

I Know it was The

BLOOD

That Saved Me

BY

Tay M. Clark

ISBN: 1530583268
ISBN-13: 9781530583263

IN MEMORY OF

My father David E. Clark, my mother, Mrs. Mildred B. Clark, and my maternal grandmother, Mrs. Lillie (Green)Mason, you'll forever live on in my heart.

12-21-16
Amazon
15.$\underline{^{00}}$ (card)

B
C5496i

Table of Contents

Acknowledgements

I have been inspired by so many to write this book, but most of all by my Heavenly Father God. He is the Author and Finisher of my faith! He is also my Keeper, and truly He kept me, as I lived the message of this book. I want to thank Him for seeing and believing in me, when I failed to believe in myself and did not see myself as He does. He also kept me when my faith was not where it is today. I grew through; I did not just merely go through. For I know the thoughts that I think toward you, saith the LORD, thoughts of peace, and not evil, to give you an expected end. Then shall ye call upon me, and ye shall go and pray unto me, and I will hearken unto you. And ye shall search for me with all your heart. And I will be found of you, saith the LORD: and I will turn away your captivity, and I will gather you from all the nations and from all the places whither I have driven you, saith the LORD; and I will bring you again into the place whence I caused you to be carried away captive. Jeremiah 29:11-14 (KJV) I want to thank my Shepherd Bishop, Dr. Keith L. Curry, for cultivating the gift of writing and creative expression through this literary form. He taught as I caught the word of God. The Logos became Rhema and came alive as the Holy Spirit through him gave me instruction, guidance, direction and even correction. I am forever grateful. If it were not for him, I would not be here today to tell the story of God's Divine Love, Mercy, Grace, Favor, Glory, and especially The Blood of Jesus Christ. I Know It Was the Blood That Saved Me! I want to thank my dear friend and Sister/Author Tumeki Griffin for assisting me in the process of editing and self-publishing this book. She literally helped me to birth and to deliver this baby. Against all odds we pressed through and I pray that it is as much of a blessing to you as it was for me to carry it and to bring it to life in book form

Preface

This book was written in obedience to the leading of the Holy Spirit and prophetic instruction to tell the story of God's glory in, over, and through my life. It tells of how God, through the Blood of Jesus Christ has kept me in the midst of life's struggles and transformed my life; for my good and for His glory. Total transformation has occurred; spiritually, emotionally, socioeconomically, relationally, psychologically, and in every aspect of my life. It literally became my life line so that I may live life, and that more abundantly. I do not know where I would be if it had not been for the Blood of Jesus that was shed on Calvary for me! I am grateful and I love him for the opportunity to tell the story of his glory in my life. *I Know It Was the Blood That Saved Me.*

Introduction

This book is about my personal transformation through the process of being transformed by the renewing of my mind. Washed, cleansed and covered by the Blood of Jesus, I was renewed by the reading, hearing, understanding and application of the word of God and being taught the significance of it and the importance that it had in transforming my life.

It is about having a sincere and genuine relationship with Jesus Christ as my Lord and Savior, Brother and Friend. It is not just about having "fire insurance", to escape hell, but to escape and avoid the penalty of sin, guilt, and shame; to have life and that more abundantly; as promised in the word of God; the Bible.

It is not as much about what has happened to me in life that makes the difference, as it is what has happened in me, as a result of the Blood of Jesus covering my life. It has caused me to become even more rooted and grounded in His love and the word of God. The Logos became Rhema.

The process was not easy, but it was well worth it. God is truly the Author and Finisher of my faith and this book. I am just the scribe who wrote what He inspired me to write. Knowing that God is the One who began this process of transformation; " Being confident of this very thing, that he who has begun a good work in me is faithful to complete it until the day of Jesus Christ." (NIV)

I am determined, I have a made up mind, and I am fully committed to walk with Jesus all the way, come what may, because He walks beside me, and I am never alone. I owe him my all. He gave his all so that I might live. I Know It Was the Blood That Saved Me!

Was my faith always where it should have been? NO, but God! His grace, mercy, loving kindness, long suffering and patience were always with me. He never gave up on me and He would not let go of me. I, on numerous occasions wanted to give up and even give in, but God knew just what to do to keep me, and I thank God that He kept me. Yes, He kept me!!!

I have been reminded that the race is not to the swift, nor the battle to the strong, neither yet bread to the wise, nor yet riches to men of understanding, nor yet favour to men of skill; but time and chance happeneth to them all. (Ecclesiastes 9:11)

For our light affliction, which is but for a moment, worketh for us a far more exceeding and eternal weight of glory; While we look not at the things which are seen, but at the things which are not seen: for the things which are seen are temporal; but the things which are not seen are eternal. (2 Corinthians 4:17, 18)

I pray that as you read this book that you find something that ministers to your spirit and to your soul, enabling you to receive and apply the word of God in your right now situation. God knows and sees where you are and He cares about and loves you. He says in His Word, "Beloved above all things, I wish that you prosper and be in health, even as your soul prospers." (3 John1:2)

He enabled me, through His Holy Spirit and the Blood of Jesus to adapt, adjust, and to overcome.

1

He Saw the Best in Me

I thank You Father God that you saw the best in me, but even more importantly, you sent the Man of God; Bishop, Dr. Keith L. Curry who saw the best in me, when everyone else around me could only see the worst in me. He took the time to search beyond the external, to see the internal and eternal; spiritual me. He saw my strengths and weaknesses, but encouraged me to fast and pray, study and to apply the word accordingly. He encouraged me to be the best that God has called me and assigned me to be. I thank God that giving up was not an option. Bishop, Dr. Curry challenged me to excellence in the kingdom of God for my good and God's glory; even when the odds were against me. He believed in me, even when I did not believe in myself. I was unsure of my ability. I had allowed the voices of the external influences dictate to the internal; which God himself had placed within me. It was about God's ability and my availability, obedience and faithfulness. It was when I knew for sure that God had called me to this assignment and that He was going to see these promises fulfilled; that I knew I had to follow it all the way through and no more hiccups. Focus and fight through the distractions. My fight for victory became stronger than the opposition. I recognized it for what it was and was trying to do to me and my destiny. All I said was, you picked on the right one this time Satan. It is on. I bow to no one but Jesus and God.

He taught me how to stand strong in the face of adversity, pray and fight; without wavering. He taught me how to bleed, but not bleed out onto others while I was going and growing through. He taught me how to seek God's face all the more and for His answers to my questions and not man. He taught me by example how to enter into the presence of God as I worship and praise Him for His goodness, mercy and grace; and his loving kindness. He taught me that weeping may endure for a night, but joy comes in the morning. It is morning time! But as 1 Corinthians 13:13 states, "And now abideth faith, hope, charity, these three; but the greatest of these is charity. Charity in this scripture, meaning love. God, through Bishop, Dr. Keith L. Curry taught me more than anything else how to love myself and others when things did not look like what God had promised and they showed jealousy, envy, hatred, scorn, disrespect, disbelief in who God says that I am. I learned to love them, because I knew that they did not know what and to whom they were doing what they did. They really did not! If they had known then, what they know now, they may have chosen differently. I don't know. I am responsible for what God charged me to do and I have learned to stay in my lane and leave others alone. I will pray for them and not prey on them. God has it all in control.

Bishop, Dr. Curry took the time to cultivate me and to study me as he heard your voice Father God and studied your word. He instructed me according to your will, way, timing, purpose and plan. Abba Father, I thank you.

Just as you have Father God: he looked beyond my faults and saw my needs and enabled me to see it for myself and to believe and receive all that God intended for me to have. Bishop, Dr. Keith L. Curry taught me to not settle for less than what God intended and purposed for me. I may not deserve it to many, but God's love, favor, mercy and grace says that I can. Jesus paid the price, and so, I want all that I am entitled to as a joint heir with him and as a child of the

King. Jesus suffered, was persecuted, betrayed and scourged. He hung, bled, was stretched wide and died for the sin debt that I owed and could not pay. By his blood I am atoned for and justified. He rose again on the third day with all power in his hand and the keys to the sting of death, hell and the grave. He did all that so that I might have life and that more abundantly. Do you really think that I would settle for anything less than what God says that I am entitled to? Excuse me please, step aside. I am going to get mine and after all the hell that I have been through. I know that His living and resurrection was not in vain and neither has the investment that God has put into me been either. I shall have what He promised me and the gates of hell shall not prevail against it. I am my Father's child. He who has begun a good work in me is faithful to perform it until the day of Jesus Christ. *I Know It Was the Blood That Saved Me!* Father God, I thank you for my Pastor and Bishop, Dr. Keith L. Curry.

2

A Silent Cry

How many times have we looked at others on the surface and they seemed and appeared as though everything was fine with, and for them? How many times have we passively said, "they are alright and they will get over it", or " they need to get over it"? Do you even know their story? Do you know what they have endured?

Much of what they have had to endure is because of their circumstances; the things that surrounded them in their environment; things due to circumstances beyond their control. You have not a clue in most cases what that truly and fully entails. It is not wise to judge a book by its cover, because, you do not know what lies deep within the pages, and or its intended message. One must take the time to read the book thoroughly first; sometimes more than once. There is something that you are bound to miss, misunderstand, or even misinterpret the first time you read it. Even better, you do not know the charge that God has given them and he is counting on their obedience and faithfulness to fulfill the assignment that he preordained and predestined. Things are not always as they seem to be.

I must say that I personally have gone through this and I allowed others to define me by who they thought that I was. This cornered me, but caused me to come out fighting. My fight was not against them, but their ignorance. It caused me to take a self-assessment of not who I thought that I was, but who God says that I am. I did not have a clear picture of who I am, because I allowed myself to be defined and invalidated by my shortcomings and not who I am as created by God. I had to learn what the word of God says about me, and that I am fearfully and wonderfully made in His image. I had to learn through experience that He loves me enough to protect me and keep me, even when I can't see my way clear. When I would do wrong, God would block me from my own self. LORD, I just want to say, Thank You!

I found myself wanting to, and feeling the need to explain myself, when in essence I did not owe an explanation. I am who I am, because God made me who I am. I know that I am not perfect, but I am the perfect me, because can't nobody be me, but me.

Imitated, but surely not duplicated. I like who I am and I am happy in my own skin. I am not fake, and I do not try to be something or someone who I am not. It is what it "I","S" is! Love me as I am. Granted there is much room for improvement, but I do the best with what I have and who I am. If God is happy with me as I am, why should I trip off of someone else? I don't and won't anymore.

I am learning my intrinsic value and that which is being cultivated in me through the Holy Spirit and the help of God and his manservant; Bishop Keith L. Curry. There is more to me than what meets the natural eye. I will not cry another tear because I do not measure up to what someone else thinks that I should be, or that I should have what someone else thinks that I should have. I do not go along just to get along. I am not desperate. I have walked alone for some time now. I like being by myself, especially if it means that I am not around drama, pretense, confusion and deceit or manipulative individuals. Please don't take meekness for weakness.

God has kept me and brought me through a lot and I am still standing. Standing strong and tall as I know that he is leading me in the way that he would have me to go. He is leading me to his preordained and predestined destiny for me. It is for my good and for glory *His* purpose and plans shall be fulfilled. His will, not my will be done.

How many agree that for the most part, we as a people take into each new situation, our own personal perspective; as a result of our own personal experiences? Do you agree also that the more limited your experiences, the more limited your perspective is? You have heard the saying, "broaden your horizons", or even to "be open minded." Limited thinking does produce a limited perspective, or frame of reference. You think what you know, and /or have experienced. Therefore, it is said that we should learn to, "think outside the box."

Use our imagination and seek beyond what we know and have experienced personally. Sometimes adjustments need to be made to our current mindset, in order for us to be effective and not affected. It should be a lesson learned; if not, we shall repeat it. We need to influence our circumstances to change as necessary, and not allow it to keep us bound or limit us to what we currently are living. We are not our circumstances. We may be experiencing them and living in it for the moment, but it is not our final destination. We should not look like or identify ourselves by what we are going through. Prime example is a failed relationship. Failure may have occurred in the relationship; most often the individuals must take a realistic assessment and take responsibility for their part(s). Then there may have been a loss of a job. In either case, neither circumstance identifies the person(s) involved as a failure or a loser. It is their experience and not their identity.

Ultimately this should be a launching pad to spring forward, or a stepping stone to step up to what God has in store for you. One should not resign to a place of complacency or stagnation. There must be zeal and a fire to move on to what is intended for you, and to not settle for anything less. This is the season for excellence and not mediocrity. I have been at that level far long enough and frankly; I hate it. I had to hate it enough to put faith into action. I had to learn what I did not know so that I could do what I have not done; to obtain what I have never had.

I had to come to myself, realize and understand this for myself, because the enemy was trying to get me to identify myself as a failure and a loser. Once I came to the knowledge of the truth, the truth set me free in my mind, and my resulting actions from what I knew, believed, and put into action. I had to remember *Whose* I am and who I am. I had to remember my lineage, both naturally and spiritually.

In the natural I came from a family of progressive and prominent individuals in our community. I am proud to be a part and a descendant of such nobility, but I learned along the way that as one relative expressed to me, that, I must learn to "pull myself up by my own bootstraps."

From a spiritual perspective, I have been adopted into or grafted into the lineage of Jesus Christ, which is that of royalty. I am a joint heir with Jesus Christ and a royal priesthood. My Heavenly Father is God the Almighty and Sovereign One. I have been living beneath my privileges far too long. It's time to make a change and that change began with working with what God has given me. This book is a taste of what God has bestowed upon me and within me. I am looking forward to discovering my full potential and developing or cultivating it. It is our life assignment to do so.

Life is God's gift to us and what we do with our lives is our gift to God. What shall you render to Him?

I learned that anything worth truly having, and that I would appreciate, is worth working for; and not being handed to me. You learn the value of a thing or person when you pay the cost. In the case of a person, they then know how much you value them as well. What cost are you willing to pay for them? That is cost in time, talent, treasure, effort, patient endurance, sacrifice, etc... Think of Jesus and ask yourself, what are you willing to pay to be a true believer, and follower, or disciple of Him? He paid it all for us on Calvary. He thought that we were worth it; enough to die for.

When something is handed to you and you do not recognize or appreciate the process by which you obtained this thing; one tends to take it for granted. You do not know the cost someone had to pay. I understand and appreciate the saying of the sacrifice of "blood, sweat and tears." I am reminded of what Jesus Christ did for me long ago on Calvary. He experienced the blood, sweat, and tears, as the time approached for his agonizing torture and sacrificial death on the cross. The human side of him thought of the process by which he would have to endure and the anointed side of him enabled him to endure the cross. You and I would have never made it that far. Some of us might have lost the ghost, let alone gave it up; enduring the cross and all that preceded it.

He sacrificed his life yet while we were still in our sins. He did it once and for all. He paid the price that includes the past, present, and future. He knew that we would fall, but he loves us that much. Through the Holy Spirit we are given the power to get back up again. God forgives us when we truly are repentant and we must also learn to forgive ourselves and move forward.

The thing is how much do we love him? Ask yourself this question and take a good and honest look at yourself. This is not to condemn you, but for you to realistically assess where you are in relationship to the One whom you call your Savior and Lord; Jesus Christ. All have sinned and have fallen short of the glory of God. We must have a repentant heart and be not just sorry for what we have done, but have a Godly sorrow; one that convicts us or pricks our conscience enough for us to reverence God and make the necessary changes.

When we sin, we crucify Jesus Christ afresh. It is as if we were the ones who initially hung him on the cross. If you really think about it, we were the ones who hung him on the cross. He had us in mind and loved us enough to atone for our sins and to redeem us from the penalty of sin. He did not have to do it, but he did. He was the only sacrifice that God would accept as propitiation (substitute) for our sins. He endured and sacrificed what we should have and could not.

This brought mankind's reconciliation back to God the Father. This put us in right standing with God and justified us; just as if we had never sinned. That is why "Jesus is the Way, the Truth and the Life, no man cometh to the Father, but by me."

This does not give us authorization or the right to sin, but it does cover us when we do. It is not a matter of if, it is when. Sin is ever present with us. We can't do it without the help of the Holy Ghost. "It is not by power, nor by might, but by My Spirit", says the Lord.

"Let this mind be in you that was also in Christ Jesus. His

thoughts are not our thoughts and His ways are not our ways. His thoughts are far above what we can even think or ask." We are limited and God is limitless in all things. I have learned that if I do not know, ask God for wisdom and understanding. Do not try to flounder in a thing until you make it; wasting precious time and energies; frustrating oneself. Oh, how well I have learned. Time and energy are precious, especially if you are bombarded on every side already. You will find that as you mature, you realize that you may not have as much time in front of you as you do behind you; therefore appreciating and cherishing each moment.

Think beyond what you have experienced and or can see with you natural eyes. We have to learn to have a vision and think beyond our personal limitations. We have to learn to expand our horizons and take off the limitations of our thinking. "As a man thinketh, so is he." We limit ourselves and our possibilities by how and what we think. We often go no further than that what we think or know. There is so much more, outside our own, personal frame of reference. That is why I believe that in the word, that it says, "My people perish because of lack of knowledge." The other saying is,

"Without a vision, the people perish."

It was not until I learned to look beyond what I could see naturally, that I realized that there is so much more for me to have and that I had to reach beyond my norm or comfort zone to conceive, believe and receive what God has for me. How did I know that it existed? You have read the scripture that says, "Eye has not seen, nor ear has heard, nor has it entered into the heart of man, what God has in store for them that love Him." There is something that I have not even imagined or considered. Why is that? God is that great and he is limitless. We limit ourselves because of what we think of ourselves, our past failures, and disappointments. We have also allowed ourselves to be limited because of what others have said, or have thought of us.

I learned to break loose and shake myself loose from what others thought of me, because they do not know me and even if they did, what God has planned for me is far greater. Only He validates me. I am just learning the full potential of Tay M. Clark.

I once did not dare to venture beyond the norm, because of

fear of the unknown and past failures. Life, I have found out is a risk, whether you choose the risk, or by passivity; it is chosen for you, by others or circumstances. Why give anyone that much power over your life? That belongs only to God. Live life to the fullest and trust God. He will keep you as you follow him.

This is the voice that he gave me and I am using it. I shall no longer remain in silence; nor cry in silence. Thank you, Father God and thank you Jesus Christ. Thank you for loving me to life! A life that is so much richer because of your blood and presence.

3

<u>The Rhythm of My Father's Heartbeat</u>

Do you know the rhythm of the Father's heartbeat? Do you really? I ask that because if you did, why are so many out of sync, or alignment with the will, way, purpose, plans and timing of his will for our lives? Why are so many trying to get God to conform to what they want, instead of being in compliance with the instructions that He has given to us?

So many are out of step and out of timing to what God's will is for us. It is for His glory and not for our own self-seeking motives or agendas. God loves those who he has created and he wants to give us all the opportunity to get it right so that we may be reconciled back unto himself and to spend eternity with him. He wants us to have life and that more abundantly. God knows our heart's desire and he also knows what is best for us. What we thought that we wanted is far less than his best for us. Are you willing to wait on the Lord; for his best for you? You will know that it is his best when you have to go through hell and fire to get to it. How bad do you want it? Know that it is He that is keeping you through it all and he orders your footsteps as you trust Him. Your trust, faith and focus must remain on him to make it. There are so many distractions, but as I have read, we must, "starve our distractions and feed our focus."

With God's mark of approval, no matter what you have to go through to get to his promise for you, he will keep you all of the way and will protect and provide for you. I know, because I have had to live through it personally and I am here to tell you about his goodness, his mercy and his grace. I never would have made it without him. I am a living and breathing witness of his everlasting love. I am so glad that he loves me so. I really love the Lord.

God loves a humble spirit and a contrite heart. He loves a teachable spirit that is willing to submit to his will, way and timing. In all of this our faith is the key to what we do, in what we believe and have confidence in. We are to trust God with our whole heart, mind, body, and spirit. We must also apply it and do just what he instructs us to do; being obedient and faithful to his will and to his way; even when we do not understand. God loves, and will not do anything to harm you. Will you trust him? I do!

21

Apart from him we can do nothing, but fail. As we are in tune with, and in sync with the Father's heartbeat, we are able to sense and know when there is pending danger. We are able to sense excitement, the peace of God and his love and so much more. Our discernment becomes sharper and keener. We are able to understand better and wisely apply what we have learned.

We are better able to be at peace even when we are disappointed, because we know that God allowed it for a reason. The question that we are to ask is, "Lord, what lesson(s) am I to learn from this?" Whatever he allows us to go through is for us to learn a principle or statute of his; so that we will be more in tune with the rhythm of his nature and his voice. We will learn that it is not to punish us, but to strengthen us for what he has planned for our future.

"My sheep know my voice and a stranger they will not follow." We will know what is of God and what is not; we will be led by His precious Holy Spirit. We will not only be led by the Holy Spirit, but will live according to the Holy Spirit and not fulfilling the things of the flesh. We would be convicted and not condemned, because we know that God chastises those whom He loves. Aren't you glad to know that he loves you; I am?

This all comes as a result of being in relationship with the Lord and spending time with him in prayer and meditating on the Word of God. Our desire should be that we are in harmony with God. That sounds glorious, and I pray that as we do come into alignment with God, his assignment for our lives, and in sync with His heartbeat that we will be more Christ-like and Kingdom minded. "So as a man thinketh, so is he." We are Kingdom of God citizens, and I pray that you will believe and receive all that he has planned for you, with your name on it. God bless you!

4

<u>A Sip From My Grandmother's Saucer</u>

As a child, my grandmother would drink coffee each morning with her sweet and low and cream. That was a part of her morning ritual. Before that she would always say her prayers and grace at each meal. Every once in a while my grandmother would give me a sip or two of coffee, because she said that she could give me a taste. I did not need to be drinking coffee. She would pour a little in a saucer and allow it to cool and would allow me to sip it from the saucer. Just as she did with the coffee, she would do with the word of God and prayer. She would pour a little for me to partake of. She taught me the model Lord's prayer and she would say it with me each morning and night. She taught me the importance of prayer and showed me by example in her lifestyle, her conduct, speech and how she treated others. She was a loving soul and was always cooking at that kitchen stove. She always had something good to eat and I always loved her cooking, as did many others. She was of help in any way she could. She would encourage me and correct me if I was wrong. She knew that I liked to dance, but she would tell me that I should be somewhere praying and not dancing or I was going straight to torment. That was her way and a biblical way of saying to h---!

She took boarders in to her home to help as she could. She was the first one to show me what God's love looks like and she walked her talk. She was a fairly quiet woman, but one of strength, fairness and nobility. She dressed modestly and was always adding something to lengthen her dresses if they were too short. She sewed, crocheted and was rich in wisdom. If she was angry it was very rare. She did not stay mad for long. These are the things that I remember and I cherish those memories of her. I loved her and I know that she loved me. She showed it and spoke it in her voice and tone.

She was the first one to care for me at home after my mother birthed me, as my mother recovered from caesarean childbirth and toxemia; I was very close to her. She was that way with her children, grandchildren, great grands, nieces, nephews, her siblings etc.... Even the neighbors and community loved her. I truly received the best sip from my grandmother's saucer and that is the love of Jesus and what He means to me. I thank God for a praying grandmother and all that she taught and imparted to me; things that I did not even know that she was imparting, until I grew older. I miss her dearly; she was a Proverbs 31 woman for sure. Momma Lollie, thank you for being the vessel of honor that God used to teach me his ways! She was an angel; messenger of God! I speak personally from my experiences with her, but she loved many and each one's life was richer for it.

5

<u>A Just Man</u>

A just man is one who is justified as if he had never sinned. Now in your mind, one must be saying if one has sinned, how is it that they are seen as if they had never sinned? As a born again believer and Christian, we are justified by grace; which is the unmerited favor and gift of God. It is not obtained by anything that we have earned or deserved, but because we received Jesus Christ as our Savior; we believe in our heart and confessed with our mouth, that Jesus Christ is Lord. We also repented and turned away from our sinful ways.

We are new creatures in Christ Jesus, because, old things are passed away and behold all things have become new. Has everything changed overnight? Usually not, because there is a process through which we must go through. The heart, mindset and commitment of the believer and their obedience and faith also determine how long the process will be. How many have said that they would commit to something and would do so for a short while and then revert back to their old ways when things get to seemingly become unbearable? Well, this Christian walk is not an easy one, but it is a necessary one. It is necessary for the church today or should I say the "Kingdom Citizens," that we have a made up mind, commitment and dedication to the obedience of the Cross; obedience to Jesus Christ and the example which he set before us. We must count the cost and consider the cost of the Cross. Consider the cost of hell as well. It is not worth it! Jesus paid it all and justified us through his shedding of blood; death, burial and resurrection. Some are glad just to be saved; with fire insurance and some want to live the way of the cross, in that they come into not only identity, but relationship with Jesus Christ. We then are not the ones that cry Lord, Lord, but denying the power of the cross and his shed blood. We not just know about him, but we come to know him, intimately. He is no longer just a casual acquaintance as some choose for him to be. A part time lover, if you will. This is someone for convenience sake that can fulfill a need momentarily or temporarily, but overall they can't fit the bill or fulfill your every need. This is the way some so called Christians act. They have not fully surrendered all to Jesus. They are very selective in what they want to give to him and that which they want to keep, because they want what they want and they want to be in control of their lives and be independent of Jesus Christ.

Well, I am so glad to tell you that a Christian's life is not independent of Jesus Christ, but totally dependent and totally surrendered to him who died and gave his life that we might live, and live more abundantly. God's word says, if you love me, you will keep my commandments. Now, in saying that, God knew that we all would fall short of keeping the Ten Commandments, and any other commandments that he has given. By the way, they're the Ten Commandments and not merely the Ten Suggestions. Many people treat them as such. For convenience sake they adhere to only that which they think that they can easily manage or control. The truth is, we as humans are and have the tendency to be fickle from time to time and in some, it is all the time. "A double minded man is unstable in all his ways and will receive nothing from God."

Saved by grace and justified through faith, lest any man should boast, it is the gift of God. No one has earned the bragging rights to possess salvation through anything less than grace. Just as no man can come to the Father, but by Jesus, through the shedding of His blood on Calvary, as the Sacrificial Lamb of God. The truth be told, our righteousness apart from Jesus is as filthy rags. On our best day, all have sinned and have fallen short of the glory of God. When you say that you have not sinned, and become proud in your own mind, there you have sinned, for one you have lied and have become proud in your heart.

In John 3:16 ~*For God so loved the world that He gave his only begotten son, so that whosoever should believeth on him should not perish, but have everlasting life.* John 3:17, goes on to say that, Jesus did not come into the world so that the world might be condemned, but that the world, through him might be saved.

This is why it is so important and significant that we are saved or born again into the kingdom of God through Jesus Christ. It was the blood that He shed on the cross at Calvary that redeemed us from the penalty of sin and the atonement that reconciled us back to God; our Heavenly Father. We have tried life our own selfish way, with us at the center of our will. How do I know, because that was once me? I wanted what Tay wanted and did not consult with

God or others that had more insight and wisdom than I. Had I consulted them, especially God first; it would have saved me a lot of time, effort, heartache, headache and money. But God in his infinite wisdom, patience and longsuffering, love, mercy and grace; saved a strong willed sinner like me. You can be adamant about something, but still be wrong as two left feet as I was. Through life's circumstances, he saved me continually from others and especially myself, because it was the decisions that I made or failed to make that had led me to the pit at that time that I was in. Yes there were other factors, but the bottom line was; what had I settled for and what had I allowed. I did not know and realize then what I know now. Thank God for his saving grace that is not just one time, but continually, as long as we have breath in our body and even after that if we chose Jesus Christ as our Lord and Savior. I am fully committed and surrendered to Jesus Christ as his disciple; a disciplined follower of the way of Christ. Is it easy? Absolutely not! It was never promised to be easy, but God said that lo He would be with us always and that He would never leave, nor forsake us. He has been there all of the time and has proven Himself faithful, even when all else has failed miserably. Thank God for justification under the blood that cleanses me from all unrighteousness of sin; past, present and future. Does that give me the license, right, authority or entitlement to sin habitually; NO, it does not! Will the mercy of God continue to cover me? Only as long as He knows that your heart is right and that your intentions and motives are pure. You can fool others and yourself, but you can never fool God. So a word to the wise, get right kingdom of God citizens and repent, while you still have a chance; in your right mind and amongst the living. Time is short and God is looking for those whom he can show himself mightily in and through. Are you justified by the blood of Jesus today, or will you make that choice to get it right, because the next moment or day is not promised to you?

I know it was the blood that saved me, once and for all eternally! Will it be you today? Are you tired of being tired, have you come to the end of your rope and have suicidal tendencies? Are you at a place of being overwhelmed, and you don't know which way to turn? Does life seem like there is no use anymore? Have you come to the end of yourself? Please, try Jesus Christ. He will never lead you wrong and even in the tough times, he will be right there to see you through. How do I know, because he has been there all of the time for me? He has kept me in my right mind and did not allow me to visit or entertain suicidal thoughts or anything of that nature. Did the enemy try to tempt me with that ideology, surely he did and it was immediately dismissed, because I was reminded of Whose I am and who I am in Jesus Christ? As a child of the King, those thoughts are not even an option, not even a fleeting thought as the enemy would have you to believe. The devil is a liar and I don't entertain his life draining thoughts. Remember, he only comes to steal, kill and destroy. Jesus came that we might have life and that more abundantly. Choose ye this day whom you shall serve. Choose life or death. Where will you spend eternity when you close your eyes permanently?

6
He Was There All of the Time

How many know and realize that God was there all of the time? In and out of time, He was, is and will always be there. His presence is as he states in the word; *I Am, that I Am*; that is whatever you need for him to be at that given moment or space of time.

"I would have fainted if I had not seen the goodness of the Lord in the Land of the living."

I thank God that this world is not our home and that we are just passing through. It is wicked and things have gotten digressively worse; deteriorating the fabric and morals of life and our sense of peace, happiness, right, wrong, and safety. By that same token, it has challenged and forced many, such as myself to hold to God's unchanging hand. What we have depended on for so long is no longer dependable or our source of safety or viability. It is no longer our firm foundation, but God is, and God is shifting our focus and confidence and who we depend on.

I have learned that, "I can depend on God. Through the

storm, through the rain, through the sickness and the pain; I can depend, I can depend, I can depend on God!"

That is one of my testimonial songs and it holds a special place in my heart, every time I hear it. It speaks volumes of truth, because I can relate and identify with what it is saying. There is no doubt in my mind, in him, of his capability to see and bring me through and or out of the storms or struggles of life. My assessments and reassessments rest in whether or not I am in the right position, and posture to receive what He is demonstrating in the spirit, or in the earth at this time. Position yourself, your mind, body and spirit to receive all that He has planned for you to receive. Don't miss your blessings following something other than the voice of God. If you're following the voice of the Man/Woman of God that is in authority over your life, be sure you follow them as they follow Jesus Christ. It will line up with what God is saying and will confirm what God, through his Holy Spirit has already spoken to you or is speaking to you.

That is why you must be in relationship and know God for yourself personally. It is not good enough to just know about God,

Jesus Christ, and Holy Spirit, but you must come into the revelation, relational and experiential knowledge of each one and the significance they have in your life.

Knowledge is power and it is what you know that will empower you to stay, stand, and step on out there through your faith. Stay in prayer for your leaders, because they too; sometimes make mistakes and need support and encouragement. Just as they are there for us they would like to know that we are there for them as-well. They're covered by the Blood of Jesus too. We're to love them, say that we love them, and cover their nakedness. We want ours covered, don't we? I did not say condone that area of weakness or struggle, but to pray that they will come to the knowledge and understanding of, and line up with what the word of God says and what the Holy Spirit is leading the church to, in this day and time. Take it to God and no one else; leave it there.

God is watching, because he allows things to happen, to see what we as the church will do. If you fail the test, you are bound to repeat it. Love your neighbor as yourself. Love does cover a multitude of sin. It is to cover those that are trying to do right, but have not gotten it right yet. God sees and He knows. He is counting on us to give by demonstrating the love, mercy and grace that we have received from Him.

Look back over your life and recognize the areas that God was at work on your behalf and still is. Each day that you wake up is another sign that He is not through with you yet. The truth be told, every time you got something that you know that you did not deserve or when you did not get what you did deserve; he was at work. When he blocked that or those bullet(s), when he did not let you die from whatever you were involved with illegally or immorally; He was at work. When He kept you in your right mind and you know that you should have lost it, and many have, under less distress. Thank God for His loving kindness, mercy, love and grace; it is His Keeping Power! There is no one that loves us like He does, nor can they.

Don't grieve the Holy Spirit and/or the grace of God. At some point, God will leave you to yourself and He is not mocked whatsoever a man sows, that shall he also reap. He warns us and corrects us, but some take his grace and mercy for granted and abuse it. Woe unto those who do.

God has been there all of the time. He reminded me of His goodness. He watched over me when I felt alone, even when I felt desperate, when I felt forgotten and rejected and even when I went without. He was there when I lost a baby to miscarriage at 3 months of gestation. When I lost my house to forfeiture and a household of belongings because the person that I was connected to did not recognize or value what God had given me, whose I was in Him and what He wanted to do in my life. Be careful of who you connect to!

I say this as a testimony of what He has kept me through and in spite of it all, I am still here and in my right mind. I survived and so can you. He taught me to put my hope in things eternal and not on things that can be lost and that the moth can corrupt. Things and people come and go, but only that which is done for Jesus Christ shall last.

He has never left me nor forsaken me. He has been there all of the time, since birth and since the first day that I turned my life over to him and accepted Jesus Christ as my Lord and Savior. He kept me, protected me, healed me, and provided for me. He reminded me that yes, He has allowed me to walk through some hard and difficult places in life, but that was only to strengthen me and to prepare me for what lies ahead in His predestined plans for me.

He was there when I was molested as a child, when I was raped as an adult, when I was emotionally abused, antagonized and intimidated. He was there when I was beat in my head for no reason known to me other than the person allowed anger to control them. From which resulted bruises that it hurt to put my head on the pillow. It would have been worse accepting I felt the protection of the angels that surrounded me. It felt as though I was being covered and although I felt the force of the hits, it was buffered and not the sharp force I would have felt if I were not protected at all.

I remembered the person becoming angered because I dared to fight back and I did not back down the way they wanted and had hoped that I would. He was there for me to deliver me out of that environment through my son.

He was there when my Toyota Van began to smolder in

smoke and Holy Spirit told me to close the windows, turn off the vehicle, grab your purse and warn your passenger to grab what they had and get away from the vehicle. We went safely to the sidewalk close by. It was raining that day and we were sitting at the red light with several vehicles in front of us and we had to get out and leave the vehicle. No sooner than we had gotten to the side walk, we looked back at the vehicle, only to see it go up in flames. The flames rose so high that I thought that they might touch the telephone lines that were above it.

He was there when he awakened me out of a deep sleep on two separate occasions to alert me to begin to pray for my oldest son, not knowing at that time that it was the prayer that would save his life and cover his life with the blood of Jesus.

He was there when those whom I was supposed to be protected by, I needed to be protected from. He was there when those who said that they would help me and knowing my situation and vulnerability would manipulate and control the situation to suit them. He was there when I was down to Ramen noodles and I knew how to make it work for my family and I. He was there when I lost my mother and when I lost my father. He was there when I was threatening to miscarry with my second child and was considered to be at high risk. He was there when I was in a house during the hot month of June and July with no electricity, for 8 weeks in the house and I became nauseated on several occasions. I found out months later, when I had to go to the emergency room because of a respiratory ailment; that my heart was seen in the x-rays for a chest x-ray for my lungs; to be enlarged. The Dr. told me then that it is a good thing that I did not have a stroke when I was nauseated in the heat and that my body was warning me then; when I became nauseated. He covered my family and I.

I did not know then what I know now. I did not know how much fight there was in me for survival. Through all of this I prayed, and I kept calling on Jesus and said in my mind and in my spirit, "Lord; I don't believe that this is what you meant for me or my children. If it be your will, please deliver me through or out of this so that I may live and do better for my children. I learned that fight was in me and it surfaced as needed. I thank God for deliverance. He empowered me to be wise as a serpent and harmless as a dove.

He was there through the numerous times of homelessness when I was married and once I separated and was divorced. He was there in the times of transition.

I am not here to point the finger or blame anyone for what has transpired, life happened and I have forgiven others as well as myself for the choices that were made. They were lessons learned and wisdom acquired. Lord I thank you for your Keeping Power through it all.

I did not always know and recognize it for what it was; a tool or vehicle to get me to where he wanted me to be, spiritually, mentally, emotionally, physically, relationally and even financially. It is giving me the right to exercise the authority that He has given me. For I have been tried, tested and found to be true. Surely, it has caused me to cling to him even more than ever before; like a little girl holding onto her daddy's legs. I sought to be closer to Jesus and I grew in him and he in me more than ever before. I truly learned what being transformed by the renewing of my mind and through the blood of Jesus meant. I lived and survived it.

Father God has reminded me that my destiny is already written; hence the terms predestined and preordained. He has let me know on several occasions that it is a done deal. The Victory was written in the story line long ago, even before I even realized that there was a story line. It is not so much what has happened to me as it is what has happened within me that matters; transformation through the Blood of Jesus Christ. I have learned that we overcome by the word of our testimony and the blood of the Lamb, I am a living witness.

As my illustrious Bishop, Dr. Keith L. Curry would say, "It is a fixed fight." The story line is one of victory and not of failure. I may have failed along the way, but I am not a failure, nor are you. I must trust God and walk with him in faith, love, and in confidence that He will do what He promised he would do. I believe God! I shall stay the course, running on to see what the end is going to be. My name is Victory and I Know It Was the Blood that Saved Me!

It was and still is for me to realize and to be obedient and faithful to His instructions to me, and to follow it as if my life depends on it; and it does. Not only does my life depend on my obedience and faithfulness to God, but that of so many others that are waiting for me to line up with the calling that God has placed on my life. He has allowed me to transition through life to learn of His goodness and that He is still the same, no matter what I go through or face. He is the same, yesterday, today and forever; and he changes not. His methods in which he accomplishes a thing may change, but his character, principles and statutes do not. He is Holy, Righteous and Sovereign. He is so much more, but words alone cannot truly express all that He is and has been to me. God is my everything.

He is not caught by surprise by what I have had to go through and to endure, He wrote the story and I am just one of the chosen characters in the story. He is the Author and the Finisher of my faith. He says to be strong in the Lord and the power of His might. He says to be strong and be of good courage; do not fear. It is not by power, nor by might, but by My Spirit, says the Lord. That means that it is not by my power or efforts, not by my might, but by His Power, His Might and His Spirit only that Victory is won. Anything less than that does not assure victory in Jesus and He is not obligated to put His stamp of approval or blessings on it. God has supernaturally and sovereignly orchestrated and controlled my life and I am learning to recognize, have faith in him and not waiver in my belief, thoughts, or actions; not to worry unnecessarily. That is even when all hell breaks loose and things look chaotic, trust God.

I had to because when things seemingly spin out of my control that is the prime opportunity for God to step in work and on my behalf. You know when opposition rises against you and you have done what you know to do and things still go astray. People look at you sideways and wonder what is wrong with you and you look back at them and tell them that you did the best you knew how to do. It is a setback, to be set up, to go up in Him. After you have done all to stand; therefore stand, putting on the whole armor of God to stand and fight against the fiery darts of the wicked one.

I dared to believe what God says about me and to trust Him no matter what, it was not easy, but it is well worth it and I am and shall be who and what God says I can be and was created by him to be. He is in control and I surrendered my control to Him. He's got it all in control and He was there all of the time.

Can I tell you this, even when I knew what I was capable of and had accomplished these things before, I began to second guess myself, because of what others thought about me. Instead of me relying on the truth and God, the enemy of my destiny wanted me to believe his lies and antics to try to persuade me and others to think the worse of me. I took my eyes off of God and began to sink, does that sound familiar? Even as an ordained and licensed evangelist, I was second guessing myself, I had to be reminded that even though I do not wear the title currently, I know who called me and that I was licensed and ordained February of 2013. The anointing was still on my life and is what kept me through the time of testing and conditioning. I felt like Job and somewhat like Jesus. I have been reminded, if I suffer with Jesus, I shall also reign with him.

This walk and commitment is not for the faint hearted, so if you cannot take chastisement, correction or rebuke this is not for you. If you are not willing to lay aside your own personal agenda, will and plans, this is not for you. If you have wishbone and not Holy Ghost backbone, this is surely not for you. If you cannot live a life of no compromising of God's standards, this is not for you, because

He will hold you accountable and responsible. To whom much is given, much is required. It is about being about the will of the Father; being the church and the spiritual hospital for the sick, lost and captives. Lead from the front by example. Adopt the lifestyle of sanctification, holiness and righteousness, without which no man shall see God. Ask yourself, Am I willing to go through the process to prepare me to be used by God for his glory and magnification? Also ask yourself this, Am I the example that I want others to follow and to glorify God which is in heaven? Count the cost! It is costlier if you don't though! At least through the process you can say that, He was there all of the time.

Thank you Abba Father God and Jesus and I love you with everything that is in me. I reverence, honor, and praise your Holy name. I pray that my life glorifies you, because you are worthy to be praised. Life is your gift to me and what I do with my life is my gift to you. Thank you for the transformational power of the Blood. Father God; thank you for choosing me and even more so for loving me. I pray that you are well pleased! Thank you Jesus for the Blood, for I know it was the blood that saved me

7

<u>The F.I.G.H.T.</u>

I realize now that I have had to fight all my life in one way or another. Coming into the world I fought to live and throughout my early childhood due to childhood illnesses. I have fought for what I believe and have known to be right morally and spiritually. I was taught at an early age about spirituality and have applied it as I understood it. God was preparing me then. I have been in the church all my life and it was not until I came to the understanding of what being born again and being in relationship with Jesus Christ was; did I fully understand what it all meant. I am still in the learning process and it is never ending.

I was seventeen when I got saved. Little did I know that was the beginning of the F.I.G.H.T. for me as I know it today! **Fierce In God's Holy Transformation**. Today I am Fully in God's Holy Transformation. The difference being that I came to the knowledge of the calling on my life and because I answered the call, I am fully committed to the purpose and plan that God has for me.

The fight began the day that I answered the call. The enemy attacked me in my sleep and my cousin informed me that she overheard me telling the adversary that I do know my 10 commandments. Even then the adversary knew that there was something special on the inside and his job was to kill, steal, and destroy it; in whatever way he possibly could. He started by trying to put doubt and fear into my mind and to distract me. I did not know then what I know now and I was easily distracted and in ignorance to the full word, principles and statutes of God. I was not aware of the significance of the Blood of Jesus, as I know it now. The process of the transformational progress has been slow and steady and it is well worth it. God does all things in His timing. I can see, and say that now, but back then, if I had known what I was going to encounter in my daily Christian walk, I may have tried to back away gracefully. My faith level was not where it is today. I am so glad that God kept His hand on my life and led me to where I am today. I would not want it any other way.

I did not know that the fight that I would have to fight would influence and save my life, my sanity, my integrity, my peace, the lives of my children and my freedom. I did not realize how important I was to God and that He had chosen me even before I was formed in my mother's womb. It was when I realized that I was enlisting in the army of God that I became a prime target for the adversary and his kingdom.

When God has a calling on your life, there is no getting around it. You can run, but you cannot hide. As good as God has been to me, I can't afford not to praise His Holy name. He has been mighty, mighty, mighty good to me and then some. Words alone cannot express all that he has been to me. I just can't explain it all. That is why you will see me in tears quite often. Those are tears that only he can understand. They are tears of appreciation, not sadness. They convey that I am so glad that I made it, and that I am still here today to tell you of his goodness in the land of the living. I survived the worse of my life and now I can enjoy the best of my life.

"I had fainted, unless I had believed to see the goodness of the LORD in the land of the living." (Psalm 27:13)

I learned that God loves me and what He thinks surmounts that of anyone else, any influence, even myself. Because I belong to him and I represent him, the kingdom of darkness is in opposition to anything that would expose or dispel darkness. I learned the hard way, but I learned and began to overcome the kingdom of darkness as I learned how to war in the spirit.

As long as I did not seek to become empowered with knowledge of God and His strategies against the kingdom of darkness, I was not a threat to the enemy. I just had fire insurance and I did not rock the boat so to speak. I am ready to rock the boat and turn the boat over. The very attacks against my life in the form of people, out of envy and jealousy became cold and callous. I have had people pray against me and wish that I would die. I have felt the attacks come against my body, mind, finances, and even my family. At the time of the attack I learned to war in the spirit to return all attacks to sender and back to the pit of hell from whence it came. I learned to war for my very life and that of my loved ones and friends. I thank God for the Blood of Jesus. It has literally saved my life. What may have killed others, God has had his hand on my life.

You wonder why I live the life of surrender and commitment

to God the way that I do. It is because I love the Lord, and my life and that of my family, friends and loved ones depends on it. I do not play when it comes to God and the Kingdom of God. I love what He loves and I hate what He hates. I stand on the word and will not waiver. I have become like the tree that is planted by the river of living water. I shall not be moved. I have been conditioned to stand for what I believe and know to be true, especially in the kingdom of God. After I have done all to stand, I will still stand and see the Salvation of God. He will fight your battles, if you let him and stay out of His way. I have learned that as well. God is good. I thank Him for his compassion, love, mercy and grace. He has been good to me and I can't help but to praise and worship Him. He is worthy to be praised and worshipped. He has been good to my family and loved ones. I pray for them and I know that God is a keeper and He is Sovereign.

Because I am peculiar to many, I do not fit in, therefore I am a misfit and I have learned to be alright with that. I don't want to fit in. It is not conducive to what God has for me to do anyway and I do not feel comfortable. I have learned not to go along to get along.

I do not have to and I do not want to either. What God has for me, it is for me and it will be so much better for me. I have just learned to wait on God and allow Him to shift the circumstances and situations in my life for them to line up with His purpose, plans, will, way and timing for my life. I am alright with that and it was not always that way.

As I was enlightened by the Holy Spirit as to what and why the things in my life are the way that they are, I came into the knowledge and understanding of the purpose for all things. All that God allows is for me to learn to depend on Him and not other sources. God is a jealous God and He will not allow you to have any other God before Him. When you belong to God, He will not allow it. Watch and see, if you don't believe me. When the word says, "Touch not my anointed and do my prophet no harm." Take heed. God is intentional in all that he does and if you do not know the purpose, ask him and he through his Holy Spirit will reveal it to you in due time, especially as you have the need to know.

I have had to fight for what was mine and what God had already said was mine, but the enemy decided that they wanted to occupy the land. What they thought that they were doing to me, they were actually doing for me. What they thought that they were doing to bury me, they actually planted me and my roots grew deep and strong. For that, I say, thank you. You blessed me real good. If you had known that the pressure was only going to produce the promise, you would have never messed with me. That is the same thing that the adversary did to Jesus and it just pushed him to the promise and the Victory. Again, I say thank you for all that have done. I am better and wiser and I love the Lord all the more. I know so much more about Him and no one or nothing can make me doubt him.

8

Rejected By Man But Chosen by God

How many of us have been rejected by man and chosen by God? If you are going to follow the example set before us through Jesus Christ that would be just about right. It does not feel good, but it all works for our good. We do not often see what God is doing in us, through us and for us, but it is working for our good and for His glory.

Because He has called and redeemed us from darkness and brought us into the marvelous light, we are misfits to this world. We are picked out to be picked on, yet we still lose sight of our purpose and Gods' plan(s) for our life.

When one thinks of rejection we think of the worst case scenario, but that is from the world's perspective, but looking from God's view, especially His eagle's eye view it is quite promising and rewarding. You know the scripture, *"They that wait upon the Lord shall renew their strength, they shall mount up with wings as an eagle, they shall run and not be weary and they shall walk and not faint."*

This to me means that my confidence is placed in God, not in self or man. I wait for His leading and guiding, His divine instruction, because I know that He, His word and His love are unfailing. He can do anything but fail and He can't lie. So, when He says that *"Lo I am with you always. I shall never leave you nor forsake you,"* He means it.

We may be rejected by man, because they don't know our value. But God, He knows our value because we're His creation and He created us in His image, His likeness. Often we have to dig deep to find that treasure because of our fallen, sinful nature that has to be revealed as we find ourselves in Jesus Christ and our true nature comes to life. "Whenever one does not know the value of a thing they are bound to misuse or abuse it. It will most likely be used for something other than what it was intended for in a derogatory way. We have to be so deep into Jesus that we find ourselves in Him. Others are able to find us in Him as well. Apart from him we are nothing.

We are a peculiar people, unique and a royal priesthood. We are special to God and He protects His own. We are ambassadors for God and He wants us to show His love, mercy and grace as He has shown us personally. We are to be living epistles read amongst men. We must love and be bold for God. Some by nature are bold and others learn to be bold as a means of survival, such as myself. It was there all along and I had to discover it. When pushed into a corner, a cat will come out fighting to live and so have I. I shall live and not die to declare the works of the Lord.

It is all too often that because others do not understand and do not like that you have chosen to follow the way and Cross of Christ; they do not want your light to shine, because it exposes or challenges them to be more Christ like if they've professed to be Christians. Some say that it does not take all that, but I beg to differ. It takes all that and then some. If God has chosen you, you cannot do what everyone else does. You *cannot* hang around everyone, you cannot think like or say what you use to say either.

Why? Because as an ambassador for Christ, you have to represent Him. Your life is a representation of *His*; pleasing in His eyesight. It is not part time, but a full time life style; it becomes a part of you, your nature and character becomes more like Christ. You sound like, walk like, talk like and even begin to look like Jesus Christ and our Heavenly Father God. You take on His D.N.A. (Divine Nature and Anointing). It is all because of the Blood of Christ.

"I have learned that it is not so bad to be rejected by man. Man's rejection has been God's redirection to something better and protection from anything less than His best for me," says, Bishop, Dr. Keith L. Curry. We must learn to appreciate all that He gives us, but be just as grateful for that which He does not give us. He knows the end from the beginning and He knows what is best for us, even when we don't. He is our daddy and I am glad about it and that He loves me so. I am my Father's child; Abba Father.

I have prayed that God would protect me from dangers seen

and unseen and that He would close doors that need to be shut and that no man can open and to open doors that no man could shut. He has done just that and He let me know that He did just what I asked of Him. How soon we forget what we have prayed for. We fail to recognize that God's ways are higher than ours and so are His thoughts. I am glad about it. He literally saves us from ourselves. We do not always recognize it at the time and we want what we want, not realizing until after the fact that if we had only listened to His instructions and had been obedient. Obedience is better than sacrifice. It saves us a whole lot of unnecessary heartache, pain and lost time.

9

<u>A Virtuous Woman</u>
Proverbs 31:10 – 31 (NIV)

In this section, I have provided space for you to study and write what these scriptures mean to you and how they transform your life. Take time to journal as you gain new insight to what God wants you to learn and how this applies to you personally. You will never be the same.

10) A wife of noble character who can find? She is worth far more than rubies.

11) Her husband has full confidence in her and lacks nothing of value.

12) She brings him good, not harm, all the days of her life.

13) She selects wool and flax and works with eager hands.

14) She is like the merchant ships, bringing her food from afar.

15) She gets up while it is still night; she provides food for her family and portions for her female servants.

16) She considers a field and buys it; out of her earnings she plants a vineyard.

17) She sets about her work vigorously; her arms are strong for her tasks.

18) She sees that her trading is profitable, and her lamp does not go out at night.

19) In her hand she holds the distaff and grasps the spindle with her fingers.

20) She opens her arms to the poor and extends her hands to the needy.

21) When it snows, she has no fear for her household; for all of them are clothed in scarlet.

22) She makes coverings for her bed; she is clothed in fine linen and purple.

23) Her husband is respected at the city gate, where he takes his seat among the elders of the land.

24) She makes linen garments and sells them, and supplies the

merchants with sashes.

25) She is clothed with strength and dignity; she can laugh at the days to come.

26) She speaks with wisdom, and faithful instruction is on her tongue.

27) She watches over the affairs of her household and does not eat the bread of idleness.

28) Her children arise and call her blessed; her husband also, and he praises her:

29) "Many women do noble things, but you surpass them all."

30) Charm is deceptive, and beauty is fleeting; but a woman who fears the LORD is to be praised.

31) Honor her for all that her hands have done, and let her works bring her praise at the city gate.

Proverbs 31:10 - 31 (NIV)

As a Proverbs 31 woman, I know who I am, but more importantly, I know Whose I am. God says that I am fearfully and wonderfully made. I am the apple of his eye. He upholds me with his righteous right hand. I dwell in his secret place and he hides me under the shadow of his wings as in Psalms 91:1 ~ "He who dwells in the secret place of the Most high shall abide under the shadow of the Almighty, I will say of the Lord, he is my fortress and my refuge, in him I do trust." I reverence, trust and believe in him. God is everything to me and with my life and the very breath that I breathe; I will serve, honor, praise, worship and obey him. His love is greater than any love that I have ever experienced and he just keeps on blessing me. Through him, I have learned to love more and to have a heart for his people and people in general.

I seek to honor God in all that I do, say or think. Just as I wanted my biological parents to be proud of me and to be pleased with me, I want that even more with God. I want him to lead and guide me to be the best that I can be, not solely for myself, but for those that I love so much. I know that many do not understand a lot of which I have gone through and the toll that it has taken on me, but God let me know that I am to keep my focus on him and the assignment that he has given me and he has the rest. He will take care of all that concerns me. Don't judge me from what you see, because you do not know the storm(s) that God has asked me to walk through.

I am not perfect, nor do I want to be, but I want to live my life in such a way that it is pleasing to God and that I can enjoy it and be around others that will enjoy my presence and love me for me, flaws and all. I live, love and laugh hard and when I put my mind to something, I stick with it all the way. Living a Christian life, being a royal priesthood, a citizen of the kingdom and joint heir with Jesus Christ, I want to be in right standing with God. I want to be that virtuous woman and show other women that they too can live that way. The question is, how bad do you want it? If you want the extraordinary and supernatural blessings of God, you will have to seek the face and heart of God and not just his hands. You have to love him more than you love anything and or anyone else. It is a process, but it is well worth it. There is no greater love!

You have to do as it says in Matthew 6:33 ~ "But seek ye first the kingdom of God and all of his righteousness and all these other things shall be added unto you." I love him with everything that is in me and for God I live and for God I will die. I shall live and not die to declare the works of the Lord. If God be for me, he is more than the whole world against me. I am safe in His arms.

1 Peter 2:9 establishes I am a Chosen Generation, A Royal Priesthood, a Holy Nation. I am a peculiar person called out of darkness, into his marvelous light. This is the heritage of the servants of the LORD and their righteousness is from me, says the LORD. I am a Royal Diadem, precious and rare. I am a Virtuous Woman and a Diamond in the Rough. I am who God says that I am. Glory to God; Glory Hallelujah. In Jesus name, Amen

10

D.I.V.A. (Divinely Inspired and Victorious Always)

I am truly glad to be a child of the King, filled with His precious Holy Spirit and a joint heir with Jesus Christ. I am created in His image and growing more in him and his kingdom principles day by day. I am honored and blessed to be covered by the precious Blood of Jesus Christ. As a princess, a warrior, and a royal priesthood, I apply the Word of God daily. That which I do not understand, I ask the Holy Spirit to illuminate the eyes of my understanding and to give me the courage, boldness and wisdom as to how to apply it.

God has put the gift of creativity in me and it surfaces in many facets. The literary form of this book is one form of that creativity. When I say that I am a D.I.V.A., I am saying that I am Divinely Inspired and Victorious Always; in that which he gives me to do.

I trust in the Lord with all of my heart and I lean not unto my own understanding, in all of my ways, I acknowledge him and he directs my path. That is with all that I do and make plans for. I want my life to glorify God and Jesus Christ. I owe my all to him, because of the Blood of Jesus Christ that was sacrificed for me, I owe him my all. It can't even compare to his life that was sacrificed to save me from a life of guilt, shame, and the penalty of sin. For God's love and his sacrifice for me, yet while I was still in my sin; God I thank you. Jesus I thank you for laying down your life for me. It was love that enabled you to endure the suffering and the shame on the cross. I thank you for being my Lord, Savior and my friend. I am forever grateful. Words alone cannot express my heartfelt gratitude and love for what you did for me. "You took my place."

11

<u>Can't Touch This</u>

I was given an assignment by God to fulfill and whether others agree with it or like it or not, they can't touch this! They have tried by putting their mouth on what they think, not knowing that God is the One who began a good thing in me and He is faithful to complete and perform it in my life, until the day of Jesus Christ. In His Word, he says "Touch not my anointed and do my prophet no harm." Maybe they did not understand that memo. God does not play. I have learned that even if I do not understand something about another believer, if God says it, that settles it and it is wise to keep my mouth off of anything that I do not understand. One's mouth can get them in whole lot of trouble. As my Bishop, Dr. Keith L. Curry says, "You can tell the people that have been talking about you, by the things that they are going through." Watch and pray!

God chooses who he wants and will use them anyway He sees fit. He knows what He has put in us and the purpose for which He wants to use us; to show himself mightily through us and in the earth.

I am my beloved's and my beloved is mine. All the Glory belongs to God.

12

A Place of Humility

Remembering that I had prayed to God, that I may be more like Christ, I did not fully understand what it was that I was asking, and I surely did not consider the process of which I would have to go through and to endure. I asked basically to go the way of the cross; the same way Jesus walked. That is heavy, to say the least. I had not fully counted the cost, but I know that I was in it to win it and that I could not give up or quit and I could not, nor did I want to turn back. What I came from was familiar, yet I was dying in it. The future would be a true faith walk for me and I was learning to trust God and the leading of his Holy Spirit; leading me even more to be Christ like.

I went through, some times of sickness. that literally put me down for a week or more at a time. I was a true work in progress. I was stripped of what I had learned to rely on, even my job, my marriage and a stable place to live. I felt like a wondering nomad at one point, but God. When I decided to do things God's way and not my own, I was in a place of total submission to his Holy Spirit. I had to stand on the scripture, "Trust in the Lord with all thine heart, lean not unto thy own understanding, but in all thy ways acknowledge him and he will direct thy path."

God would put no more on me then I could bear, but then, what was I taking on myself? I could not be everything to everyone else and not doing for myself. I had to learn to say "no I can't", and not feel bad about it. I was totally reliant on God and could barely help myself, let alone someone else. "I had to learn to put on my oxygen mask, before I could help someone else put theirs on."

I had to get to a place where I was face to face with God and my "nasty now and now" situation and literally have to ask him, "What do I do now?" I was at a place to totally surrender, but yet I had not fully surrendered all to him. I would lay my problems at his feet, but then would pick them back up again. I thought that God needed help with a problem that I could not fix, yet I had given it to him to fix and I was trying to tell him how to fix it. Somebody surely prayed for me and I know that God and the angels were shaking their head at me. The word says that he watches over fools and babes. I unconsciously thought that I could help him, because I did not like the process. I wanted the prize but had not fully surrendered to the process, one of which would lead me to my divine destiny in His timing and in His way. Oh, "I Know That It Was the Blood That Saved Me." His love, mercy, grace, loving kindness and patience surely was what kept me.

My mindset had to change, it had to shift and as I learned where I was making my errors, God had to purge, prune, prod and push me. I was being overwhelmed and still missing the point of what it was that I was supposed to learn; so that I did not have to go around this mountain again. I had to be single minded and not double minded, because a double minded man is unstable in all of his ways and will not receive anything from God. I had to stay focused. What I thought was the enemy, was actually God stripping me of myself. I had to get self out of the way and humble myself under His mighty hand.

I would flow in the Spirit for a moment and then when things became overwhelming, I would step into the flesh, especially if I had many distractions. I had to learn like I did in boot camp in the

US Navy that I had to learn the tactics of warfare of the enemy so that I could study and prepare myself to be combat ready at any given time. This time it would be spiritual and not in the flesh.

What I had to learn and remember as a Christian is that the weapons of our warfare are not carnal, but mighty through God, to the pulling down of strongholds. Taking into captivity every thought, that exalts itself against the knowledge of God; unto the obedience of Jesus Christ. Because it is a spiritual battle, I could not use natural or carnal thinking or means to solve that which I was encountering. Once I made up my mind and was totally surrendered, dedicated and committed to the cause of the Cross through Jesus Christ, all hell literally broke loose. I did not know that I then had acquired a bulls eye sign on my mind, heart, body, finances as well as my children and marriage. I was in warfare and did not know how to fight in the spirit.

Oh, thank you Jesus! I thank God for, Apostle, Dr. Donna Payton, Senior Pastor and Founder of In His Presence Ministries. In 2010, I was in warfare in which I was not yet prepared for, but she prayed for me and with me and led me in the way that I was to go and I soon became prepared. My very life depended on it, as well as my sanctity. I thought that I was going to lose my mind and almost did. She was the one to truly train me as I was going through it; it was OJT for real. I learned what it meant to stand still and see the salvation of the Lord. I cried and I prayed, but God kept me through it all and "I Know That it was the Blood that Saved Me."

The logos (written word of God) became Rhema (pertinent, right now word). The word became the living word that nurtured and fed me as I was experiencing times of doubt and drought in my life. I wavered for a time, because I would read the word and I said that I believed it and then circumstances arose and shook my very foundation of faith. After being shaken enough, I stood flat footed and I was reminded of Whose I am and who I am in the body of Christ. I am my Beloved's and my Beloved is mine. Enough became enough and I was tired of being tired, but I was not tired enough. Not just yet. When God had promised me if I was obedient and I stood upright before him, that he would withhold no good thing from me and if I delighted myself in him that He would give me the desires of my heart. I thought that was it. Not yet my dear. Not yet.

I forgot what he had charged me to do.

He had assigned me to begin writing and I did so through my journaling. This process began over 10 years ago and I knew that I was writing, but I had not yet begun to put a book together. A lot of which, I did not think I wanted to tell anyone about. I was also going through so much that some things were so far out there that I did not even write it down and said that I would take it to my grave with me; while trying to make sure that it did not send me to my grave prematurely.

I did not think at that time that it would be my life experiences that God would use for me to minister to others and tell them how they can also overcome and conquer their situation; while fully relying on him and no one else. How they too can rely on the Blood of Jesus Christ; power in the blood and his love to see them through. He has taken my mistakes and mess and, turned it into a message and my tests have become my testimonies. The same Blood that has saved me, over and over again is the same Blood that can save you to, just trust and believe and you will receive, don't give up yet, you can be next in line for a blessing.

The other thing that I had to realize and face was that with opportunity; comes opposition. The enemy is not going to just let you have what God has promised you. You will have to answer and make up in your mind how bad do you want what God has promised you? There is someone else that would love to claim what God has promised you; even while occupying your promised land. It is sad, but so true and I have learned from experience, people can be ruthless and selfish. They become insensitive and competitive, but the thing is when you humble yourself under the mighty hand of God, He will exalt you in due season. All you have to do is show up, put on the whole armor of God as in Ephesians 6:11 – 17, and fight the good fight of faith while standing on the word of God as you operate in the will, way, and timing of God.

Being humble is actually a place of strength, so are being meek, gentle and all the Fruit of the Spirit. (Ephesians 4:1-3 and Galatians 5:22 - 23) You have allowed his strength to reign in your spirit and to have dominion over your mortal body. He is in control and it is no longer I, but Christ Jesus who lives inside of me and who gave His life on Calvary for me. (Galatians 2:20)

We must be ever so careful though, because we cannot become so haughty in our own eyes that we become prideful. We should not think more highly of ourselves than we ought to. We must edify the body of Christ and one another. Our heart, mind and spirit must be right first, not in our own eyes, but in the eyes of the Father God. It is the heart beat of the Father that we edify one another (Romans 14:19)

I pray that we each have now surrendered our will for the will of the Heavenly Father. It is about doing the will of the Father who has sent us. Not our will, but Thy will be done. Keep our motives pure and remain humble. If not, God has a way of humbling us. The word says that pride comes before a fall. The word is true. I have learned the hard way in some, not all cases and I am better for it. I am glad that He loves me and the word says that God chastises those whom he loves.

That is why the word says to, *"Humble yourself under the mighty hand of God."* Now do you understand why? It is more favorable if you humble yourself, than if He has to humble you. If you don't believe his word or me, watch and see! Aren't you tired of the results that you are getting from doing things your way? If you're tired of being tired and are at wits end, it is time to make a change. The change must begin from within. It must be a conscious decision that you make to want to make the change. It is necessary to you for your wellbeing, your soul salvation and that of your children or loved ones! How bad do you want it? How badly do you need it? Take a look at your life and to thine own self be true. Is this, the way that you are currently living, the way that you want to live the rest of your life? Be honest and real with yourself, even to the point that it may hurt. That is the point of which you are opening your soul to the leading of the Holy Spirit. A place of humility, where you can truly and sincerely say, Jesus, I need you. I have done it my way, long enough and I have tried all that I knew to do; now I want to try it your way.

If you are at a place where you're humbling yourself and surrender all to Jesus and you want to receive Jesus Christ into your life as your Lord and Savior, repeat this prayer:

Dear Jesus, I ask that you would come into my life. I realize that I am a sinner that needs and wants to be saved by your grace.

The word says that if I confess with my mouth and believe in my heart that Jesus Christ is the Son of God, that I would be saved. I am Godly sorrowful for my sins and I repent for my sins and ask for your forgiveness. Jesus come into my heart and cleanse me of all unrighteousness. I surrender my life to you, Work in me, on me and through me to do Thy will in Jesus Christ's name, Amen

I pray that you will find a local church that you may fellowship and come under the covering that you may be nurtured and trained in discipleship as a true believer and follower of Jesus Christ. It is well worth it.

I asked my cousin, "What is the fine line between sanity and insanity?" and her reply was when people expect different results by doing the same things over and over again. If you did not like the results the last time of doing something, what will make you like the results this time, unless you make a change?

'Through it all, I learned to trust in Jesus, I learned to trust in God, through it all, I learned to depend upon His word. I humbled myself under the mighty hand of God and I am so glad about it. I am so glad that I did. He kept me through it all. God keeps, covers, corrects, provides for and loves, His own.

Because I suffered with Him and for His name sake, I shall also reign with Him. All the glory belongs to God.

13

Pushed, Pressed, Provoked to Progress and the Promise
(Covered by the Blood)

Pushed

I was once visited in a dream by Holy Spirit, and in the dream, I dreamt of God holding my face in an embrace with both of His hands. I had been having difficulty staying focused on Him and I thought that I was going to lose my mind. The attacks of the enemy were steady and fierce. People were allowing the adversary to use them to push me, so I thought, but it was God allowing it to perfect what concerns me. The issue was not of being pushed, but being pushed too hard.

Little did I know that the push was my blessing, through the press, in disguise! I was being pushed, pressed and provoked to progress and the promise. I understand so much more now; the concept of God putting on you no more than you can bear and then you taking on more. In other words, biting off more than you can chew. I was concentrating more on the circumstances at hand than I was on Him and His presence in my life. I was stretched too thin and not maintaining the necessary flow to come out of the *"stuck"* that I was in. Such as in the use of a camera, microscope, or telescope lens; I needed to refocus. I needed to readjust to what he wanted me to focus on at that given time; He was and currently is to be my main focus. For God says in The Word, that He would keep my mind in perfect peace if I keep my mind stayed on Him. God let me know on numerous occasions that no matter what disappointments or difficulties come my way, to remember that I am His daughter.

Distractions come, but at the time of that distraction, when the adversary would want to use it against me; God has enabled me to recognize, shift my thinking, refocus on what mattered the most, and continue on in the task or assignment that is set before me. That primary task at hand is to write and finish this book. It has begun to work in my favor, because it literally catapulted me forward and it gave me more determination to get past these obstacles or hurdles.

Instead of the rock falling on me, I chose to fall on ***The Rock,*** which is Jesus Christ; the Anointed One who shed his blood on Calvary for you and me.

Press

It's a press at this time, because I have to press past current conditions and circumstances, and see in the spirit what lies ahead; or better yet, remain calm, as I steadily hold the hand of the One that knows what lies ahead. I trust Him more today than the day before. Through experiential knowledge, it has enabled me to be truly blessed; empowered to succeed. As I forget those things that lie behind; I am truly in a press towards the mark of the prize of the High calling in Christ Jesus. I also realized that "behind", is that which occurred as recently as a second ago. It is in the past if it is behind me and I must lay hold of what is before, or in front of me. All that He has promised, and purposed for my life, lies in waiting for me to fulfill; that which He has called me to. I once thought that I was waiting on God, and learned that Heaven is waiting on me to fulfill the last assignment given to me; before I can effectively move on.

From the outside, looking in, it may seem as if I am not doing anything, but contrary to popular belief, my mind has been constantly going, sometimes overwhelmingly so. That is when God tells me to come into His Presence and rest. I have been trying to accomplish it in my own might; it was not meant to be that way. In my effort to get it done I was relying on myself; when it is God who gave me the assignment. I trust Him. I believe God.

"From the end of the earth will I cry unto thee, when my heart is overwhelmed: lead me to the rock that is higher than I." (Psalm 61:2)

When enough becomes enough, and you get tired of being tired; one musters up all the strength they have to do what's in their power, but then realizing that it is not by power, nor by might, but by my Spirit, says the Lord. Jesus is the Captain of this ship and God is the Author and Finisher of my life, my faith, and this book.

Like an artesian well, I was being pumped and pressurized to produce the necessary flow and to stay in the flow of God's Spirit to finish what He has started in me. When I say that God is the Author and Finisher of my faith; I mean that in many more ways than one.

I am in an uncomfortable place, because I know there is more for me, and it is mine for the asking and for the possessing. This is not the final destination, but a pit stop to where God is taking me. It is a stepping stone and a part of the process; a thorn in my side, if you will, that will push me to overcome all hindrances and obstacles through staying in the presence and processing of God. I first had to overcome in my mind, heart, and spirit, so that I could overcome in all other areas of my life. When life has given me lemons, I have learned to make lemonade; Jesus being the sweetener!

I learned that I was not to become comfortable, passive, or stagnant in the place of mediocrity, or less than enough, because I was on my way to the place of more than enough, abundance; my promised land! Through it all, *I Know It Was the Blood That Saved Me.* Others are counting on me and that is why it is imperative that

I finish this project. I did not want to die in the wilderness, nor did I want to kill or forfeit my promise or the assignment that God has entrusted me with. My purpose is greater than my pain.

The scriptural reference of (Matthew 6:33) *"But seek ye first the kingdom of God, and his righteousness; and all these things shall be added unto you."* comes to mind, and is ever before me; therefore, reminding me to keep my priorities in order and to not be double-minded, but to be single-minded; standing on, believing, and trusting what God has said to me. Having unwavering confidence and faith in him, and not what others have to say or do, especially those without authority or jurisdiction in my life. For in being double-minded, I would receive nothing from Him. Single-mindedness is the call for this season. Anytime you want to receive from God, you must believe when you ask; having confidence that he can do what you are asking of Him and even more so, what he is asking of you. The question in many of our minds is, if He will! What has he told you already? Learn and know what God's will is for your life. In knowing God, you will learn the character and nature of God. You must develop a relationship with him. He will keep you in perfect peace as you keep your mind stayed on Him. Trust and do not doubt, for He will work it out!

As we, (kingdom minded believers of God) oftentimes say, "Won' he do it, Won't he will?" The answer is a resounding yes. He will do above and beyond what we can ask or think. God is searching for who He can show himself mightily through in this hour, and season of our lives. He has called us, but will you be chosen? It depends upon your level of dedication and commitment to the call, your obedience and faithfulness. Will you answer? Now, do you understand why many are called, but few are chosen, and even fewer are considered? Look at Job's example. Are you willing to lay your life down to the extent that Job did and still say, "though you slay me, yet will I trust you?"

Anything that is contrary to his word; you will know that it is not from God. I have learned that God can and will use circumstances or people to fulfill his will. So, any time that you want to hear from God, understand what to do; not necessarily why to do, but what to do; be stirred up in your most holy faith; press into His presence like never before. Pray and fast to hear from him and he will answer. What does the word say, and what has he already done in your life and for you? Think on it and let it marinate in your spirit, mind and heart. I pray that your faith fails you not in the process. It is truly not for the fainthearted, for you shall reap the reward if you faint not. *"But seek ye first the kingdom of God, and his righteousness; and all these things shall be added unto you."* Matthew 6:33 (KJV).

Two other scriptural references come to mind and they are, (Psalm 37:4-9 and Proverbs 3:5-9), which states the following:

"Delight thyself also in the LORD; and he shall give thee the desires of thine heart. Commit thy way unto the LORD: trust also in him; and he shall bring it to pass. And he shall bring forth thy righteousness as the light, and thy judgment as the noonday. Rest in the LORD, and wait patiently for him: fret not thyself because of him who prospereth in his way, because of the man who bringeth wicked devices to pass. Cease from anger, and forsake wrath: fret not thyself in any wise to do evil. For evildoers shall be cut off: but those that wait upon the LORD, they shall inherit the earth." (Psalms 37:4-9).

"Trust in the LORD with all thine heart; and lean not unto thine own understanding. In all thy ways acknowledge him, and he shall direct thy paths. Be not

My son, despise not the chastening of the LORD; neither be weary of his correction: *"For whom the LORD loveth he correcteth; even as a father the son in whom he delighteth. Happy is the man that findeth wisdom, and the man that getteth understanding."*

In other words, simply put God first, before anything else. Whatever you think and, or endeavor to do, your motives for thinking or doing a thing should stem from wanting to do the will of God, and to please Him. This is primary, and anything that results from it, is the overflow, or secondary to the principle thing. The principle thing is to be in the will of the Father and to be covered under the blood. Not my will, but Thy will be done. I then say, Lord, please let it be on earth, as it is in heaven. That it would be peaceful and glorious; thereby glorifying Him.

I also learned that anything that is not in His will, is not covered under the Blood. That would be anything that one does in disobedience to what he has told you to do or not to do. He is not obligated to keep it. If you want to be covered, be sure to be in alignment with the will of the Father; His assignment for your life. He gives us free will, but he also lets us know that there are consequences. We must choose ye this day whom we shall serve. What has he called you to, or what did you call yourself to? Know the difference and you will save yourself and others a lot of heartache, trouble, effort, time and chastisement or curses.

Anything that we want or desire and it is not initiated by, commanded by, or called forth from God, now enters into the realm of witchcraft, because it is now against or in opposition to the will of the Father God; it is now classified as disobedience to the will of God. God's word speaks in Jeremiah 29 of the captivity in which he has carried away captives (verse 4). He goes on to say inverse 7 "Seek the peace of the city whither I have caused you to be carried away captives, and pray unto the *LORD for it: for in the peace thereof shall ye have peace.*"

(Jeremiah 29:11-14) For I know the thoughts that I think toward you, saith the LORD, thoughts of peace, and not of evil, to give you an expected end. Then shall ye call upon me, and ye shall go and pray unto me, and I will hearken unto you. And ye shall seek me, and find me when ye shall search for me with all your heart.And I will be found of you, saith the LORD: and I will turn away your captivity, and I will gather you from all the nations, and from all the places whither I have driven you, saith the LORD; and I will bring you again into the place whence I caused you to be carried away captive." (Jeremiah 29:11-14)

14

Pain That Produced the Promise

Just as it is in giving birth in the natural, so it is in the spiritual, it was pain that produced the promise. After going through for so long and not seeing the final product or the promise, I began to become frustrated and anxious. When am I going to have some relief, when is this going to be over? Or as the old song goes, "When we gonna get to the good part?"

As I was going through, I did not always know what was to be expected as a result of the process of going through. I knew that I was pregnant with a purpose for God, but I was not sure what the outcome was to be. It was prophesied to me, on more than one occasion that I was to write; producing books from my life experiences. Why did I hesitate? Well, writing is not where the hesitation was, because that part of the process began immediately. I believe my hesitation was in what to put into the books and what was it that God wanted me to share with my reading audience? Who was I to address, what was I to talk about and surely, how was I to put it all together, to produce the book(s) that I was assigned to do?

Where were the finances to come from to promote this project? I was distracted. I was now getting in God's business, not a good place to be, I promise you. I learned that he does chastise those whom he loves. My job assignment was to write the book. The key is to do what he says to do and when he says to do it. If you don't know how to carry out what he has assigned you to, ask and you shall receive the answers. Pay attention when you ask, because the answer will come in ways that you least expect sometimes and other times it is right in front of your face.

We must watch and pray and some things only come with prayer and fasting. You will soon learn what those some things are. It also depends where your faith level is. You may need to fast and pray so that your faith level will increase. It is imperative that you become a part of a local assembly and are covered and fed the word consistently and regularly; on a daily and weekly basis. That is if you are truly committed to God and Jesus and do not just want, "fire insurance."

We as disciples must learn how to follow the leader(s) that God has assigned us to and to be groomed properly in the ministry. We must know what the will of the Father is for us and follow accordingly. In order to learn to lead, we must first learn to follow. This is one of the first places of learning to humble ourselves.

My job was to write in obedience to God's command. It was not a suggestion, but a command that was to be executed immediately at the time it was spoken. In disobedience, I hesitated, not in rebellion, but in fear, because I had never written a book before. I did not realize at the onset, that what God had given me the vision to do, that He would also give me the provision to fulfill it. I did not know that then. The thought and scripture comes to me. "My people perish because of lack of knowledge." It is for me to follow instructions, "Trust in the Lord with all thine heart and lean not unto thy own understanding, but acknowledge him in all thy ways and He will direct thy path. Obedience is better than sacrifice! It personally affected me and therefore became a pertinent part of my life story, struggle, and testimony.

I found out, that my job was to just write what Holy Spirit

gave me and use the creativity that God has given me to share with my reading audience what I have experienced in hopes of making a difference in others' lives. I have a voice and messages that resulted from what I have endured and survived. What God has done for me; He can do for you.

Sometimes it would be just one word, and sometimes it would be a short statement, or an idea that would later be expounded upon as I began to write.

I began journaling as a result of having gone through so much. I needed a means of release and I was experiencing migraines and having symptoms of high blood pressure, having anxiety attacks and feelings of hopelessness; feeling as though my life was out of control. When I first began journaling I was married. I wanted to write, but was afraid that my inner most feelings, now on paper would be discovered and used against me by my ex-spouse. I remember now that it began as simple as writing down the things that I had on my to-do list. As I completed each item, I would check it off. It was therapeutic for me and enabled me to regain some sense of control of my life. It was manageable and I could see what I was dealing with, when, what some of the triggers were for my migraines, anxiety attacks, feelings of hopelessness, feelings of loss of control in my life etc…

As I was able to identify the causes and effects of each of these things; I was then able to seek answers to the questions that arose. I had strayed away from spending as much time with God in prayer as I once had. My priorities were not in order and I had to reassess where they were, and what I needed to do to get them back into order. I had to reassess my time and priorities and make the necessary adjustments. I needed to learn how to manage once again. God wanted me to spend time in His presence once again; as I had before.

Even then it was the blood that saved me. As I attended church, it was my life line to survival and to make it from day to day and Sunday to Sunday. I would not miss church service, unless I was so sick that I could not make it. I remember one time that even though I was sick, I still went to service. I could barely make it, but I managed to make it in and during service, I began to feel better. I am so glad that I did not give up or give in then. I had perseverance and determination in my spirit; bulldog tenacity is what I call it. God knew what He had placed in me and would not let me give up. *I Know It Was the Blood That Saved Me.*

"Nobody, but you Lord, nobody, but you. Nobody, but you Lord, nobody but you. When I was in trouble, you came to my rescue. Nobody, but you Lord, nobody, but you".

He has always been a very present help in the time of trouble. There are things that only God knows, because I would not talk to anyone about them and because it is a thing of the past, I can leave it right there, but God knows and it is because of His Son Jesus Christ's blood that I made it. My children have been covered by the blood as well and I am so glad about it. I know that my obedience to praying for my children has spared their lives on many occasions; protecting them from dangers seen and unseen. It was the blood that saved us.

Looking way back to even my own birth, had it not been for the Lord on my side, and my mother's; neither one of us would have made it. I am so glad that God knew me before I was conceived in my mother's womb. It was then that my late maternal grandmother; Lillian (Green) Mason prayed for us to make it and to be healthy. I thank God for the prayers of the righteous, for they availed much.

One thing I can look back and realize is that my marriage had not been initiated, orchestrated, nor ordained by God, but it was used by God as an instrument to make me who I am today. We were living in his permissive will, even though married, because that was what we wanted and he allowed it. I can now look at it through the eyes of maturity and say that it is not regret, but a lesson learned and because of what I have gone through, I am a better, stronger and a wiser person for it.

Much healing has had to take place as a result of the things that were endured by all involved, but God is a Healer and he has and still is healing all brokenness, hurts and wounds; psychologically, emotionally, socially and spiritually. Even after forgiving, healing has had to occur. As I read the word and applied it accordingly to my life, it began to heal and cleanse me from all unrighteousness and heal the wounded and brokenness; it began the process to making me whole again. I had to learn to truly forgive others and myself; let go and let God. Only He would be the One to heal, set free and deliver me from the hurt of my past.

Once I separated and divorced, I was given a new start; I wanted to be all that God wanted and called me to be. I really wanted to be God's woman; Proverbs 31 woman. One who sought him daily and wanted to learn more about the Kingdom life. It was time to move forward and I did not know where forward was for me. Making it one day at a time seemingly was a struggle for the longest, but God, through his Holy Spirit led me through and to where I am today. It has been a long and tedious journey, but He has led and kept me all of the way; that is why I am still standing and still here to write and tell about it. *I Know It Was The Blood That Saved Me.*

I embarked on a new journey of faith with Holy Spirit in the lead back in July of 2007. I learned who I could trust and who I could not. Who was there for me when others weren't, who had hidden agendas, who literally wanted to see me dead and out of the picture, who were laughing at my struggles, especially during the times of homelessness and displacement. Who thought that it was funny when I was working only part time and that I could not afford to always do what others could and would do etc....

God had those that truly had my best interest at heart in the picture. Then there came a time that I asked God to show me who people truly are and that anyone that was not conducive to the plans that he had for my life too sever them from my life. There came a day that God showed me that he was the one that let me go this route for a reason. He led me into a place of captivity so that only he could bring me through and out of it. It was to be used for my story, but primarily for His glory. There were times of betrayal and the sad part was, those that betrayed me, did not think that I knew and they would smile in my face and say, Hi Sister Tay thus and so. Little did they know, He was there all of the time. *I Know It Was the Blood That Saved Me.*

It was the pain that produced the promises of God, because it pushed me to greater. It caused me to develop even in the darkest of times, when I thought that I was going to lose my life and my mind, but God. It put a fight in me stronger than ever before. I have always been a survivor; but only God could have brought me through what I have gone through. I would not settle for less than what God intended for me and I would not allow anyone or anything to stand in my way of the promises of God, not even myself. It was through the pain and suffering that I learned to keep my focus on God and not my circumstances. I learned to listen to the voice of God, watch and pray more intensely, move in obedience to his instruction and to remain committed and faithful in my church attendance, tithing and offering.

I learned the difference between the facts and the Truth of God's Word. God is in control and He is the Author and Finisher of my faith. I thank God for the Man Servant that watches over my soul and covers me in prayer; my Bishop, Dr. Keith L. Curry. I truly believe that if I had not listened and been obedient to the leading of God, I would not be here right now. I thank God for His love and protection, his loving kindness, mercy and grace. Through it all God kept me!!!

I learned most importantly that, "My Purpose is Greater Than My Pain," as taught by Bishop Keith L. Curry. God has been grooming and preparing me for greater in His Kingdom assignment. It has been imperative that I be faithful and obedient to the instructions given through my pastor and Bishop. It has been literally a matter of life and death.

What God has for me, it is for me and it does not matter the opinions of others. On lookers and naysayers are not privy to the assignment that God has on my life and therefore have no say or hand in the process. All the negativity has just made me more determined to stay focused on God and to ignore ignorance. Many times I have said and will continue to say, Father forgive them, for they know not what they do. If God be for me, he is more than the whole world against me.

15

<u>Discerning a Seasonal Change or Shift</u>

There are conditions in our lives that are uncomfortable, but yet we tolerate and endure them for the time being; it is temporary. In the meantime, we try to do what we think is necessary, to move forward, up and out of that place into that which is favorable and destined by God. I liken this to the proverbial rusty nail situation. You know, that place where there are conditions that are unfavorable, but you tolerate them? You must know when that place is not to be tolerated, but is also toxic to you and unhealthy in all aspects of your life (mentally, emotionally, physically, spiritually, socially, economically etc....) There are then also, circumstances that are never meant to be comfortable or favorable from the very beginning; just a stepping stone. It is not a place to settle, but to prepare for where God is taking you next. I am in such a place now.

An indication that enough has become more than enough, is when you cry yourself to sleep at night and ask God to help you to endure and to overcome; and press past the circumstances;

especially when your body begins to react to the stress that you have endured. When the fire is turned up and the adversary would have us to think that it is meant to consume us, but yet it is actually sent by God to cause us to move and shift in the flow of His Spirit; as He had designed for us to do from the beginning. It is meant to strengthen and mature us; a part of God's plan. While in this place I discovered that there are others counting on me to make that move, because me being in this place is affecting them as well. Those that are attached to you and that love you will provoke you to change, expeditiously; I might add.

This is a springboard place, where your back is against the wall and you come out fighting; strength under the control of the Holy Spirit. Your life depends on it and so does your mental and emotional well-being. This temporary setback is your place of comeback. What is in you is bound to come out and to overflow, either positively or negatively. Who or what you allow to be in control of your life and to influence you at this time, is the determinant as to who is glorified at that moment. What you feed the most will be the strongest as well.

I choose Jesus and ask continually that the Holy Spirit would help me to continually overcome and to become better and not bitter. My thinking had to shift first. *"As a man thinketh, so is he."* It was said in a message given by my illustrious, Bishop Keith L. Curry, who preached, *"You are better than that."* Because I am connected to such a visionary, I have to shift when He shifts, in the Spirit and in my mindset.

I had to see my value and self-worth from God's perspective, therefore adapting my mindset to that of someone who is worthy of what the King of Kings has to offer. Christ in me is the hope of glory and his righteousness justified me; just as if I had never sinned. By grace through faith are we saved and not of works, lest any man should boast. Through repentance and forgiveness; by adoption, I was grafted into the Kingdom of God; through Jesus Christ and the blood that he shed on Calvary. I am a child of the King, therefore making me royalty; of royal ancestry. I am a joint heir with Jesus Christ.

Christ in me is He who has made me worthy; as I am covered by His Blood. I could no longer settle for that of a paupers or peasants' mindset. A place of settling and mediocrity; no more! Not because of who I am, but because of Who He is; Jesus Christ, the Son of God.

I can no longer brush my problems away in fear; I must address the things in my life that are beneath the standards of God. God did not give us the spirit of fear, but of power, love and a sound mind. Know your place in the Kingdom of God. Anything less than what God intended for us, or has called us to; is literally a slap in his face; as taught by my pastor, Bishop Keith L. Curry. If he is the King and you are His child; you need to recognize who and whose you are. As Vickie Winans says in her song, *"Shake Yourself Loose."* There is another song that comes to mind; "It's Time, Time to Make a Change, We Are the People, We Can Do It." No more trying, it's time to "Just do it." Obedience to what God has told you to do is better than sacrifice.

Don't let the things of life infect you to change, but rather affect you to become more effective. My motto is, "Life is God's gift to us, and what we do with our lives, is our gift to God." What shall you render to Him? He does love us to life and that more abundantly. Step up, because God is depending on us to be the ambassadors that He has called and chosen us to be. Others are looking and relying on us to become what we are supposed to be, so that we can lead from the front as leaders and affect the change in the body of Christ. People are hurting and dying because they need Jesus and don't even know it yet, or how to come to him. The enemy has lied so much to them, put blinders on their eyes, and has influenced them to become callous; hard hearted.

There are many that are coming into the house of God and we must be prepared to make a victorious, overcoming difference in their lives as well as our own. We must be able to model what Kingdom citizens and Kingdom living looks like. We must first overcome to be effective and credible in the leading of those that need it in their lives. One can't tell anyone anything with credibility if they personally have not overcome or have been successful in their own struggles or walk with Jesus Christ. We have to be first partakers of the Word of God. Yes, we are all in the process and we have not arrived but as Apostle Paul says in the word, ~~ Philippians 3:12-14 ~~~

"Not as though I had already attained, either were already perfect: but I follow after, if that I may apprehend that for which also I am apprehended of Christ Jesus.

Brethren, I count not myself to have apprehended: but this one thing I do, forgetting those things which are behind, and reaching forth unto those things which are before,

I press toward the mark for the prize of the high calling of God in Christ Jesus."

God will let you know through his Holy Spirit when it is time to make a shift or change. He will forewarn you so that you can prepare in advance. He will prepare you for it, and you must watch and pray, ready to make the shift at the appointed time. Follow the leading of the Holy Spirit. Trust Him. Be about our Father God's business!

16

Not My Will, But Your Will Be Done

Not my will, but your will be done Abba Father God. I surrendered my life to you totally so that I may live in victory. I have counted the cost and I am willing to go all the way with you by my side. I do not know all that it entails, but I know that you will do what is best for me and will not allow me to be harmed. Going and growing through is a part of the process, being tried in the fire to purify, refine and fortify me for your use Father God.

I have had to move numerous times, not knowing that it was all a part of God's process. He would send me into a place to let his light shine and to cause me to trust him even more. It was in the valley of life that I grew. It enabled me to appreciate the mountain top experiences and to know that he was there all of the time. He never left my side. He sent his angels to protect me also. His Holy Spirit was there to protect my spirit and my mind. What might have killed or destroyed others; only was a means of strengthening me. The difference being, that I trusted and leaned on God and his word, and applied it accordingly to every situation in my life.

I even at one time did what "Mrs. Clara" did in the movie *War Room*. I wrote scripture on paper and tacked it to my walls in my room. I made my room my War Room; my sanctuary if you will. I needed to know what God said about my circumstances. The scriptures were added to my arsenal as I put on the Whole Armor of God. When I was faced with temptation, depression, frustration, disappointment, hurt, anger, abuse (verbal or physical), I would shut down and dig deep into the word of God. I truly do understand the song, "In the Word of God, I Found a Hiding Place."

I stood and boldness began to rise up in me and I asked God to let his will, not my will to be done in any given situation and to show me the way to go. He did. I asked him to open doors that needed to be opened and to close doors that needed to be closed. Some of them needed to be slammed shut and I asked him to give me the strength to overcome the hurt and to be able to forgive so that I could be free in my mind, body and spirit. He did. It took me a while to grasp the forgiveness part, because the adversary wanted me to continually rehearse in my mind and my heart what had happened to me and what was done to me and who had done it. All of that was a lure to cause me to be stuck as a victim and not a victor. I had to learn to be powerful and not pitiful, as Joyce Meyer speaks of. You have to be one or the other, you cannot be both simultaneously. They both took energy, one I found to be unhealthy and the other was healthy and life giving and not sucking the life out of me. One held me as hostage to my emotions and feelings. I wanted to be free and as I attended church regularly, hearing and reading the word, praying and fasting; like an onion, the layers of everything was being peeled away. The healing process began. I cried many a tears. I should own stock in "Kleenex" tissues.

What really set me free is when I thought of Jesus and His life, suffering, shedding of blood, death, burial and resurrection. That put everything into perspective, because now I was learning that if I am to reign with Christ, I must also suffer with him. It was now for his name sake and that my living was not in vain. As Jesus said to the Father God, "Not My will, but Thy will be done." If I am to identify with him, I must do so all the way and that is a cost that I was willing to pay. I said Yes Lord. He did it for me and I could do it for him. With the help of Holy Spirit, I am here to tell my story. Nothing but the Blood of Jesus has kept me and that is the God's honest truth. For those that even know a portion of my story, they say, Tay you have really been through a lot. I don't know how you do it and you keep the faith. I tell them simply, nobody but Jesus could have kept me and brought me through, in my right mind. He walked with me and talked with me all along the way. He rocked me in the cradle of his arms and gave me a peace that surpasses all understanding. For that I am truly grateful. That is why I love him so and will do anything for the LORD. He is precious to me. The more he shows me that he loves me, the more that I want to show him how much I love him. That is done through the life that I live and how I live it; putting on more Christ like characteristics, not in deed only, but in my mind and in my heart.

One day "I want to put on the robe and tell the story of how I made it over. I shall wear a crown." I felt the Holy Spirit, just as I said that. God knows, only God knows. I don't understand everything, but I am so glad that I made it. I survived and I am a living testimony of the goodness of God, Jesus Christ and Holy

Spirit. I need all three, yes I do!

What has transpired in my life to this point was from the adversary's perspective an attempt to discredit, discount, disparage and or disappoint me and to kill me. It has been the very dirt that was needed to make this rose grow and to create a diamond.

A failed marriage, a miscarriage, mental and physical abuse, intimidation, manipulation, deceit, betrayal, lies, persecution, sabotage, misunderstood, misjudged, mistreated, rumors, talked about, rejected, neglected, homelessness, unemployment, loss of possessions but not my life or my mind etc.... If I did not have a problem, how could I have known that He could solve them? It was good that I was afflicted. The word says that many are the afflictions of the righteous, but the Lord shall deliver us from them all. I felt shame and felt as though I was a failure because of all of what I had gone through. But one day, I asked why Lord, what did I do so wrong? My Bishop said that God is not punishing you; He is preparing you for what is yet to come. God asked me, will you trust me? Yes LORD, there is no other help that I know. My very life depends and depended on Him.

It is a matter of perspective. What tried to bury me, only planted me and rooted me even deeper and wider as I came to the knowledge and understanding of the word of God that pertained to my life circumstances. It fortified and nourished me, causing me to flourish. Even in the winter months of my life, while in hibernation, I was growing. God applied his spiritual "Miracle Grow" on me and my life. Believe me when I tell you that I was well fertilized, continuously.

I thank God for a Kingdom mindset shift. I was thrown in the pool of life and made to choose between sinking or swimming. Of course I chose to swim. Sinking was not an option. When I became tired, I was able to float (Fully Lean On And Trust) and rest in God; knowing that he was keeping me.

God knew when I was becoming weary, because He would tell me, "I have seen what you have gone through, I know what has come against you and what you have endured. I hear your cry and I see your obedience and faithfulness. Come unto me and rest and I will refresh you and lead you in a way that you know not of. "Will you trust me?" Yes Lord, I trust you and with my whole heart, I not only trust you, but I will also obey and be faithful, the best I know how. He reassured me that I am his and he would never leave nor forsake me. He told me to be strong, do not fear and be courageous. He has also told me to stay still on occasion and to be quiet. He would tell me that I am for you and I will see you to victory. This is My will for your life, trust Me!

I have learned that the order in which you do a thing and your level of obedience and faithfulness, determines your rate of success. I learned to seek the Creator and not the created and to stay in the flow of his Holy Spirit. God also reiterated for me to stay present with him. As is stated in Matthew 6:33 But seek ye first the kingdom of God and all of his righteousness and all of these other things shall be added unto you.

As I stayed in the presence of God, there was such a peace and a joy which lifted the weight of my circumstances and lightened my burdens. It gave me a release that enabled me to disconnect from the weights of life and to tap into the serenity of his presence. I could hear him more clearly and I could think more clearly; the clutter of my mind was gone at that moment. It was not that the issues of life had disappeared, but he reassured me that he would lead and guide me in the way that I should go. I needed only to trust and obey, have faith, watch and pray. He would even tell me what to take notice of. He let nothing come upon me unaware. Even when something was about to occur, he would forewarn me and tell me that he did not want me to be a part of it, because he was not in it. He warned me to stay clear of negativity and confusion.

I often thought that I was being rejected and that something was wrong with me. Not so. He was setting me aside for a specific use and that he wanted to protect me. I did not always understand this and it was not until my mindset shift took place did I realize this. As my Bishop has taught us, "What you're going through is not to harm you, but to strengthen and prepare you for what God has in store for you in the future."

When you know that what you are experiencing is to glorify God, it somehow gives you a different perspective and the strength to endure. You get that "I can do this" attitude. Attitude does determine altitude. Lord I just want to thank you, for being so good to me!

I would have fainted if I had not seen the goodness of the

Lord in the land of the living. Thank you Jesus! I never could have

made it without you Lord! I Know It Was the Blood That Saved Me!

17

The Puzzling Periods of Preparation

Have you ever experienced something that you were given to do, such as an assignment, a new job, life experience etc....; that you did, but while completing the task before you; you asked the question, "Why do I need this?" You may have even said that, "I will never need this." How often have we said that in classes that we took in school or college?

It was a part of the curriculum and it was planned out for a given field of study and a particular purpose. There were electives that you could choose, but they all had something to do with furthering your education in a particular field of study. You saw the individual parts or pieces to the puzzle, but could not always see how it all fit together and the significance that it had for your life.

I have learned that God knows the end from our beginning and he knows the plans that he has for us and the best way for us to process to progress. That is why his word says to, "Trust in the Lord with all thine heart and lean not unto thine own understanding, but in all thy ways acknowledge him and he will direct thy path."

He knows and sees the entire puzzle because he created it and he created us! He gives us a free will and hopes that we will seek him for the answers and the guidance we need to realize, accept and follow the plans that he has for us. How often do we do our own thing; only to find out that our own thing brings less than favorable results?

I don't know about you, but as you mature and have had life experiences that did not put you any closer to your dreams then when you began in life; you begin to reassess some things. You realize that you do not know all that you need to know, to get the desired results. If wise you will seek answers, beginning by asking God what are the missing pieces to this puzzle?

As you begin to trust God and follow his leading and guidance, you will find that he only wants the best for you, and will not allow you to settle for anything less. He gives you free will, but he will steer you clear of pitfalls. The thing is, will you listen and obey him? You are his child and he wants us to represent him in holiness and righteousness in the world. He wants to be glorified through your life. He created us in his image and he wants the world to know that we belong to him.

As we take on the characteristics of our heavenly Father, we become ambassadors for him. Trust God, for he will not lead you wrong. Even when you do not understand the process, believe that he knows you better than you know yourself and knows the whole picture, when you only know what you see and understand. His wisdom is infinite and ours is finite and limited by our frame of reference; our experiences and learned knowledge. He is omniscient; all knowing.

We oftentimes need a change of perspective; a mindset shift. Learn to see things from God's perspective; that only comes as a result of spending time with him and asking him to lead and guide you in the way that he would have you to go. His will be done. You have to study his word, read it, meditate on it, commit it to memory and most of all understand it and the application of it to your life. Pray and fight the good fight of faith, according to his will. Only that which is done for Christ will last. In Jeremiah 29:11, God's word states:

"For I know the thoughts that I think toward you, saith the LORD, thoughts of peace, and not of evil, to give you an expected end."

The other scripture that comes to mind is, *"But they that wait upon the LORD shall renew their strength; they shall mount up with wings as eagles; they shall run, and not be weary; and they shall walk, and not faint."* (Isaiah 40:31) Thank you for teaching me to wait Lord. I learned that in waiting that I learned how to think more like my heavenly Father and have his perspective and not my own. It produced better results. I have more peace, even in the midst of a storm. I did not settle, because I learned that I did not have to. I wanted God's best, so I gave him my best. Jesus paid it all and I owe him my all.

Through it all, it comes down to having crazy faith. I believe that he will perform what He has promised. This is developed through experience of what he has already done in your life and if he did it before, he can do it again. It may be delayed but not denied, and it is all being put together in such a way that you know that it is no one but God; that could have done it. Only He will get the glory for this. God is a jealous God and he shares the glory with no one. It is all working together for my good. I trust and believe that, with all of my heart. I don't mind waiting anymore, because I know that it will be well worth the wait.

The preparation is for ministry and I can testify of his goodness, how he has kept me, reminded me to stay focused, be strong and courageous and to endure like a good soldier. He has not given up on me and I will not give up on him. All that I have endured will not be wasted and will be a testimony to someone who has gone through what I have gone through or who will go through it and they will need to prepare their minds to be battle ready; putting on the whole armour of God as in Ephesians 6:11 – 18.

Realize that Satan is doing his job daily and every chance he gets. He seeks whom he may devour. He comes only to steal, kill and destroy. We as saints and children of the Most High and Almighty God must pray and fight as if our lives depend on it; and it does. Not only does our life depend on it, but those that are looking to see the Jesus in us. We may be the only Jesus that some may ever see. Our representation in the earth matters. If you think that you are living just for yourself, you are sadly mistaken. We are servants, ministers of God. We are light in darkness and the salt of the earth. And the word states in (Revelation 12:11) – *"And they overcame him by the blood of the Lamb, and by the word of their testimony; and they loved not their lives unto the death."*

I Know It Was the Blood That Saved Me

18

Trash to Treasure

Have you ever felt anytime in your life that you have been overlooked, disrespected, misused, misunderstood, abandoned, abused, antagonized, thrown out, discarded or just trashed, because your God given value was not recognized or appreciated? Know that God specializes in recycling. He uses that which others have discarded as trash, because they did not recognize the value or worth of a person or thing and will take it, breathe into it to restore life. He will restore that which the hurt, pain and turmoil has drained from you.

He will clean you up, wash you over again in the precious Blood of Jesus and wash you white as snow. It is a process well worth going through. It does not always feel good, but know that it is working for your good and for the glory of God. Once you know the value that God has given you and how he views you, it does not matter what anyone else thinks. He alone validates and assigns value and worth to you. No one can take that from you, unless you give it to them.

You have to be confident in who God says that you are and who you first belong to, anything else or anyone else is secondary to God. That is a good thing. God looks after His own and will not allow anyone to harm you, they will pay severely if they do. He corrects anyone that touches or harms you in any way that is displeasing to Him. As long as you remain under the Blood of Jesus, you are to be handled with care.

As God cleans you up, reshapes, remolds and puts you in the furnace to remove any impurities that may have been left behind. It is also to strengthen you, making you therefore more durable and fortified. He then puts you in a setting in which he wants to show you off, because you are now his treasure and He is now able to show others what HE has done in your life and how he transformed you from trash to treasure.

Your life now is evident of the goodness of God and what His love can and will do for, in and through you. It testifies of his goodness and love. He can now show himself mightily through your life and you can sincerely say, "Look what the Lord has done." You are treasured by God and he loves you. Let the Master create His masterpiece in your life; His treasure.

Will you allow the transformation to occur in your life? Submit and commit to the process, you will not regret it. Love your life enough to entrust it to God and to let go and let him do in you, what only He can do. He can make you whole again and you can live in the peace that only He can give. There will be nothing missing and nothing broken. Let him love you to wholeness as he turns what was once thought to be trash into treasure. Love you to life and I know it was the Blood that saved me.

19

<u>How Soon We Forget</u>

How soon we forget the process through which we had to go through and still are growing through. Did we learn everything overnight? A resounding No! We learned it as we caught onto it. It was taught, but we did not always catch what was being taught. I know for myself that I did not always understand that concept, because my mindset had not fully embraced what was being said, nor was it fully in my spirit, especially from a spiritual perspective; God's perspective.

One thing that I learned that you must stay in the Spirit of God to understand spiritual things. Now he has used natural things to explain and give further understanding or clarification, such as when Jesus used parables to explain biblical things. For the committed and serious believers who are totally committed to God, Jesus Christ, His purpose for us, and the process through which we are made more Christ-like; we must hunger and thirst after righteousness and holiness for His name sake. We have to dig deeper and study diligently, asking for wisdom and understanding. With that in mind, we must die to our fleshly nature and become more spiritual attuned to the will, way, purpose and plan(s) of God. It is not easy, but anything worth having is worth fighting for. That is what Jesus did for us and is still doing as He is sitting on the right hand of God the Father, interceding for and advocating for us as we are being made whole in God through Jesus Christ.

Because it did not happen overnight in our lives, how soon we forget that it is not going to happen overnight for others either. We must be loving, forgiving, respectful, patient, long suffering, temperate, compassionate etc… It is a process for them to progress, just as it is for us. Let us not lose sight of that, because as we do, God has a way of reminding us of what we so easily forget. Holy Spirit will convict us and it behooves us to listen and take heed to what He wants us to learn. That which is not learned is bound to be repeated until you pass the test. I am a witness. I have been through the tests and have the testimonies to back it up.

Pray without ceasing for others as well as yourself and watch God work on your behalf. Be sure that you believe that which you are praying for. Be specific and strategic in what you are praying for and pray according to God's will, not our own. I will say that one more time, pray according to God's will and not our own for God's will to be done. Why prolong the process and why get chastised in the process if you don't have to? Praying against God's will is rebellion and opposition and therefore it is as witchcraft. In Him is light and there is no darkness. Let us get right church and let's go home, or at least be prepared for when He calls our number. Remember that the adversary does not want you to have what God has for you and does not want you or anyone of us to become all that God has preordained and predestined us to be, because we are a threat to his kingdom.

Jesus has overcome and conquered the world and so must we, as we stay the course and follow His lead, following it all the way to the end. We must endure and not give up. Jesus did not give up. The anointing kept Him and so did love. Those must be the driving forces that keep us also.

John 3:16, 17 – For God so loved the world, that he gave his only begotten Son, that whosoever believeth in him should not perish, but have everlasting life.

For God sent not his Son into the world to condemn the world; but that the world through him might be saved.

20

<u>What's in the Blood?</u>

There is power in the Blood of Jesus Christ

There is Resurrection power in the Blood

There is Restoration, Renewal and Revival in the Blood

There is Peace like a River in the Blood

There is Promise and Covenant in the Blood

There is Identity with Jesus Christ and in the Blood of Jesus Christ

There is a Passion and Compassion in the Blood

There is Transformation in the Blood

There is Holy Boldness in the Blood

There is Royalty in the Blood

There is Transparency and Safety Therein in and under the Blood

There is an Ease of Flow in and Under the Blood; whereas without
it, there is a blockage

There is Appreciation and Gladness in the Blood

There is Repentance and Forgiveness of sin in the Blood

There is Redemption, Justification, and Atonement in the Blood

There is Breakthrough in the Blood

There is Courage, Confidence and Blessed Assurance in the Blood

There is Affirmation in the Blood

There is Definition of Purpose and Clarity of Vision in the Blood

There is FOCUS in the Blood

There is Amazing Grace and Mercy in and under the Blood

There is Healing in the Blood

There is Deliverance in the Blood

There is Protection and Provision in the Blood

There is Cleansing and Washing in the Blood

There is Life Giving and Life Sustaining Virtue in the Blood

There are Nutrients in the Blood

There is Nurturing and Love in the Blood

There is Declaration and Celebration in the Blood

There is Sacrifice in the Blood

There is Guidance in the Blood

There is Hope and Joy in the Blood

There is a flow of the Movement of God in the Spirit in the Blood

There is Favor and Blessings in the Blood

There is the Anointing in the Blood

There is Integrity, Morals and Character in the Blood

There is Clarity of Discernment in the Blood

There is Conviction in the Blood

There is Correction in the Blood

There is Revelatory Knowledge in the Blood

There is Wholeness and Faith in the Blood

There is a Thirst and Hunger for Righteousness and Holiness in the Blood

There are Defining and Refining Principles in the Blood

There is an Urgent Press in the Blood; defining the Purpose of the Blood

There is Completion in the Blood

There is VICTORY in the Blood

21

You Ain't Representing
A poem by Tay Clark

If you are not trying to live up to God's standards and His will,
purpose, plan and timing for your life,

You ain't representing!

Are you trying to do what Jesus would do, or are you trying to use
an excuse?

You ain't representing!

Have you tried to do what Jesus would do with the help of the
Holy Ghost?

Or are you trying to get by with the façade that you've got the
most?

You ain't representing!

Have you humbled yourself before God and man?

Or are you trying to act like you've got it all together and you
don't give a d---?

You ain't representing!

Have you opened your heart to God and allowed him to cleanse
and fill it with His unfailing and undying love, or have you
forgotten that all blessings and good things come from above?

You ain't representing!

Until you realize that first it is not about you, but about the love
God gave and the blood Jesus shed!

You ain't representing!

When will you understand and get that through your head?

Jesus was bruised, hung, and crucified as he bled.

It is not our will, but His will be done.

Until you realize, understand, and apply that;

You ain't representing!

22

The *Set Me Free* Prayer

Jesus, ***set me free*** from others' expectations of me, my perfectionism that ***stresses me out***, and the fear that seems to be my ***constant companion***. Instead, would You be that constant companion? Replace my worry *with **winsome faith***. Replace my fright with ***settled joy***. Replace my striving with true, relaxing, ***peace***. Amen.

marydemuth.com

23

<u>Scriptural References for the Blood of Jesus:</u>

These are just a few scriptures that will help you in understanding the providential and transformational power of the blood of Jesus, and how it pertains to you in your Christian walk. May they help you in your Christian journey and inspire you to look further into the scriptures for your personal studies.

~~**Mark 14:24**

Verse Concepts: Blood of the Covenant

And He said to them, "This is My blood of the covenant, which is poured out for many.

~~**Acts 20:28**

Verse Concepts: Overseers, Shepherds

"Be on guard for yourselves and for all the flock, among which the Holy Spirit has made you overseers, to shepherd the church of God which He purchased with His own blood.

~~**Romans 3:25-26**

Verse Concepts: Righteousness, Justification

whom God displayed publicly as a propitiation in His blood through faith This was to demonstrate His righteousness, because in the forbearance of God He passed over the sins previously committed; for the demonstration, I say, of His righteousness at the present time, so that He would be just and the justifier of the one who has faith in Jesus.

~~**Romans 5:9**

Verse Concepts: Growth in Grace, Atonement (NT), Saved from the wrath of God, Justification under the Gospel, Deliverance from Sin, Salvation

Much more then, having now been justified by His blood, we shall be saved from the wrath of God through Him.

~~**Colossians 1:19-20**

Verse Concepts: Divine in peace, Revelation, Removal of guilt

For it was the Father's good pleasure for all the fullness to dwell in Him, and through Him to reconcile all things to Himself, having made peace through the blood of His cross; through Him, I say, whether things on earth or things in heaven.

~~**Hebrews 9:14**

Verse Concepts: Cleansing of the conscience

How much more will the blood of Christ, who through the eternal Spirit offered Himself without blemish to God, cleanse your conscience from dead works to serve the living God?

~~**1 Peter 1:1-2**

Verse Concepts: Nature and Basis of Sanctification

Peter, an apostle of Jesus Christ, To those who reside as aliens, scattered throughout Pontus, Galatia, Cappadocia, Asia, and Bithynia, who are chosen according to the foreknowledge of God the Father, by the sanctifying work of the Spirit, to obey Jesus Christ and be sprinkled with His blood: May grace and peace be yours in the fullest measure.

~~ Revelation 5:9-10

Verse Concepts: Redemption

And they sang a new song, saying, "Worthy are You to take the book and to break its seals; for You were slain, and purchased for God with Your blood men from every tribe and tongue and people and nation. "You have made them to be a kingdom and priests to our God; and they will reign upon the earth."

~~Revelation 7:14-17

Verse Concepts: Consolation during afflictions

I said to him, "My lord, you know." And he said to me, "These are the ones who come out of the great tribulation, and they have washed their robes and made them white in the blood of the Lamb. "For this reason, they are before the throne of God; and they serve Him day and night in His temple; and He who sits on the throne will spread His tabernacle over them. "They will hunger no longer, nor thirst anymore; nor will the sun beat down on them, nor any heat; ......

For the Lamb in the center of the throne will be their shepherd, and will guide them to springs of the water of life; and God will wipe every tear from their eyes."

~~**Revelation 12:10-11**

Verse Concept: Victory over Spiritual forces

Then I heard a loud voice in heaven, saying, "Now the salvation, and the power, and the kingdom of our God and the authority of His Christ have come, for the accuser of our brethren has been thrown down, he who accuses them before our God day and night. "And they overcame him because of the blood of the Lamb and because of the word of their testimony, and they did not love their life even when faced with death.

About The Author

I, Tay Monique Clark, am a native of Norristown, Pennsylvania. I am an only child of the late David Eugene Clark and the late Mildred Bernice (Mason) Clark. I was born in Phoenixville, Pennsylvania, at the Valley Forge Army Hospital.

My father was a veteran of the US Army. I was raised and educated in the Norristown, Pennsylvania education system. Upon graduation, I began my college education at Montgomery County Community College; Blue Bell, Pennsylvania. After my two years there, I transferred to Johnson C. Smith University; Charlotte, North Carolina. I graduated with a Bachelor of Social Work and the honor of the Highest Scholastic Achievement Award in Social Work, in 1983. I thought that I had chosen Social Work as my major, but throughout my life experiences, I see now that Social Work had actually chosen me. I have literally experienced what I was taught in the textbooks and I am better able to identify with appreciate and support others in making the necessary adjustments in their lives.

I am the mother of two loving and handsome young men, David and Robert. They, along with God are my reason that I press toward the mark of the High calling in Christ Jesus. God gave them to me and they have been my inspiration along the way.

I am a surviving and overcoming divorcee. God has made me better and not bitter and also forgiving. I have had, and still do have my struggles, but with the power of The Holy Spirit, I am able to manage them more effectively and not have them manage me. I currently reside in Hampton Roads Virginia and will do so until God leads me to move elsewhere. I am about my Father's business.

I have literally been there and done that, with the T-shirt, souvenirs, trophy, scars and testimonies to prove that what God allows in your life is not to kill, steal from or to destroy you, but to make you stronger and wiser. The scars are only reminders of the battles that I have endured by the grace, mercy and loving kindness of God.

These were times that I was in Spiritual boot camp for what God was preparing me for and for me. There were many who did not make it, but I thank you Jesus for your shed blood; that I am one of the ones who did. All designed to give me a hope and a future and an expected end. It all depends from what and most of all whose perspective you are you viewing your current circumstances. In this case my attitude did determine my altitude and enabled me to work with what my Heavenly Father, God gave me. It was not until I changed seasons in my life, a place of awareness that I was an Eagle and not a chicken, not a buzzard, not a peacock, nor an ostrich; that

I was able to begin to make the necessary adjustments. By nature I have the DNA of an Eagle. God's word went even further to declare it. Isaiah 40:31 ~ But they that wait upon the LORD shall renew their strength; they shall mount up with wings as eagles; they shall run, and not be weary; and they shall walk, and not faint.

I waited on you Lord and now it is my time; a time that you have called me to. I will not dull the shine of You Lord in or on my life, because someone else does not understand or agree with what or how You have orchestrated things in my life. I bow to You only, Father God. You are The Author and Finisher of my faith, life and this book. Lord, I say, Thank You!!!

A Sweet Memory

Tay Clark is my name,

Norristown is my station,

Heaven is my providing place,

Christ is my salvation.

When I am dead and gone,

When my bones have rotten,

This little book (open a Bible) will tell you all, before I am quite forgotten.

As taught by my maternal grandmother, Lillie (Green) Mason. She was taught the same when she was a child.

Thank You!

WITHDRAWN

Made in the USA
Middletown, DE
12 December 2016